As seen on *The Learning Channel...*

How To Behave
so Your children will, too!

Sal Severe, Ph.D

What Professionals Say About This Book...

"I found this to be a very valuable book. It has helped me immensely with my children."

Jack Canfield
N.Y. Times Best-selling Author
Chicken Soup for the Soul

"This book speaks to the heart of the family system - the parents. Parents must behave so their children will, too!

John Bradshaw
N.Y. Times Best-selling Author
Bradshaw On: The Family

"Your book is wonderful. Not only does it contain a wealth of very sensible and realistic information about parenting, but, in addition, your style of writing makes it a pleasure to read. Your respect for children and parents is apparent on every page as is your warmth and sense of humor."

Robert Brooks, Ph.D.
Diplomate in Clinical Psychology
Faculty, Harvard Medical School
Author, *The Self-Esteem Teacher*

"This book is concise yet comprehensive. My wife and I use the ideas with our own children. The techniques work. Whenever a parent asks me about child misbehavior, this is the book I recommend."

Neil Aaron, M.D., F.A.A.P.
Pediatrician

"This book has been an invaluable enrichment to my life-skills curriculum for at-risk students. It is better than any textbook I have ever seen. The examples are so real. It makes parenting come alive."

Cindy Wojtowicz
High School Teacher

"I have read many parenting books. This book is the best. It is easy to read and understand. The suggestions are practical - they make sense - they really work. It is an enlightening book for teachers to give to parents of difficult students. In fact, it is a great book for teachers to read, too. "

Marshall Langan
School Psychologist

"I have recommended this book to hundreds of parents and teachers. This book empowers parents with specific, positive strategies that they can begin using immediately. It teaches parents how to develop self-discipline in their children."

Mary Ann Perez
Head Start Director

What Parents Say About This Book...

"Your book makes everything so clear. I feel like a new person. My life is so much easier because my children are now so much easier to manage."

"You let me know I was not alone. I thought I was the only one with these problems. Your book has changed my life. Thank you so much."

"The stories in your book are what teach the lessons. Your book is exactly what I needed. The changes in my children (and me) have been remarkable. I am so thankful my son's teacher recommended it."

"I needed this book. And so did my daughter. We have started to hug again."

"Thank you for showing me how to stop screaming and hitting. My children thank you, too."

"My son asked me to tell you 'thank you.' He likes the new way I behave. I am a new mom."

"As I was reading your book, I felt as though you and I were having a conversation about the problems I was having with my children. I could relate to so many things you say. It was perfect for me. My children are so much better."

"I bought this book for my daughter to read. She has two young boys. Your book teaches parents what I had to learn the hard way - and it took twenty years. Your book is on target with every issue."

"My child and I have both improved. Me - with discipline. Her - with behavior"

"Your book has completely changed the way I think about my children. I like being around them now."

"Most books I read make me feel guilty. I feel like the author is judging me. Your book is different. It was comforting to read. No patronizing, just lots of great ideas. Thanks."

How To Behave
so your children will, too!

Sal Severe, Ph.D

Cover design by David Bordow.

Library of Congress Cataloging-in-Publication Data
Severe, Sal.
     How to behave so your children will, too!: a
    collection of entertaining stories and practical
    ideas gathered from real parents.
    / Sal Severe.--3rd.ed.
     p. cm.
     Includes index.
     ISBN 0-9653012-0-6
     1. Child rearing. 2. Discipline of children.
    3. Parenting   4. Parent and child.   I. Title
     HQ769.S48 1997   649.64
                      QBI97-40670

Printed in the United States.   3 4 5 6 7 8 9 10

Please note: All children are unique and this book is not a substitute for advice you may receive from another professional who knows you or your child personally.

Dedication

To those who have taught me the most
about good parenting.

My parents, Mary and Tony, and

My children, Anthony, Leah and Alyssa

"Parents need to understand that their children's behavior is often a reflection of their own behavior. That's what makes this book unique. It does not focus on what children do wrong. It teaches parents what they can do differently."

Preface

I have spent the last twenty-five years working with behavior disordered children. Some of these children exhibited emotional problems, learning disabilities, and attention deficits. Most of these children were undisciplined, or rather, under-disciplined. They were all children who did not fit in because of the way they behaved. They did not fit in school or in the community. They did not fit in with other children.

Unfortunately, most of these children did not fit into their families, either. This was the problem I decided to resolve. I reasoned that working with parents had the greatest potential. Improve a child's family life and all other aspects would improve as well. So I began sharing the experience I had learned within schools and treatment centers with parents. The results were amazing. Spending an hour a week with a child's parents was significantly more therapeutic than counseling with the child for an hour.

I soon found myself working with groups of parents. Groups evolved into workshops. Since 1982, I have been conducting parenting workshops on discipline throughout the Southwest. Over 12,000 parents have attended these workshops.

I believe that I have learned more from these parents than they have learned from me. Every time I heard a new idea or entertaining story, I would write it down. Every time I heard a solution to a common problem, I would write it down. This book is a collection of these stories, ideas and solutions.

~Sal Severe

Acknowledgments

Comments from colleagues are the strongest form of encouragement. I wish to express my sincerest appreciation to Jack Canfield for taking the time to read this book and for his guidance during the publishing process. Also, I would like to thank Dr. Robert Brooks, Dr. Neil Aaron, Marshall Langan, Mary Ann Perez and Cindy Wojtowicz for their kind remarks about this book.

The success of most books depends on getting the attention of the reader. Special recognition goes to David Bordow for his brilliant and creative cover design.

Having ideas is one thing. Articulating them into print is another. I am most grateful to Dr. Susan Krueger, Marge Scanlon and Bonnie Neal for their hours of proofreading and editing.

Thank you to the thousands of parents who have given me the positive feedback I needed to sit down and write this book. Above all, thank you to the parents and children who have shared their stories so that others may become better parents.

Table of Contents

About the Author

Dr. Sal Severe is currently the Chairperson of the Psychological Services Department for the Cartwright School District in Phoenix, Az. He has been a school psychologist for 22 years. He has concentrated his practice on children and adolescents with emotional and behavioral disorders and their families. He has also worked as a teacher, counselor, principal and director of special education. He has worked extensively with public and private schools including residential treatment centers. He has taught classes and has provided field supervision for school psychology internships for Arizona State University and Northern Arizona University. He has conducted training for the Arizona Department of Education.

Dr. Severe is currently the President of the Arizona Association of School Psychologists and he is a member of the National Association of School Psychologists. Dr. Severe has received the Golden Achievement Award from the National School Public Relations Association for his work in parent training. He has appeared on more than 300 television and radio programs. Dr. Severe and this book have been featured on the *Learning Channel's* program, *Teacher TV,* MSNBC's *Daytime*, National Public Radio (NPR), the ABC Radio Network and Fox Network's *Fox on Family*. This book has been featured in Book of the Month Club and Children's Book of the Month Club. Dr. Severe has provided parenting chats for America Online and Parent Soup. Dr. Severe is listed in *Who's Who*.

In the past seventeen years, he has conducted more than 500 workshops across the United States. He has become known for his work with schools, churches and parent organizations. He has provided training for The National Head Start Association, The National Association of School Psychologists, the Council for Exceptional Children, Tough Love, and the Hemophilia Association. Workshop themes include parenting skills, child behavior, the effects of divorce on children, self-esteem, classroom management, and instructional strategies. Dr. Severe has provided training for the Intel Corporation, General Motors, SONY, Motorola, Honeywell, Texas Instruments, Pizza Hut, NAPA, Federal Express and Transamerica Occidental.

Dr. Severe has three children who consume the remainder of his energy and time, but without reservation, provide him with his greatest blessing and achievement.

Part I: INTRODUCTION AND OVERVIEW

The children now love luxury; they have bad manners; contempt for authority; show disrespect for elders....Children are now tyrants, not the servants of their households. ... They contradict their parents ... and tyrannize their teachers.

~Socrates, c. 390 B.C.

Chapter 1

How Successful Parents Behave

Whenever I am asked if my children have ever done something I was unprepared to handle, I tell this story. Anthony was almost three years old when my spouse became pregnant. We knew it was vital to prepare him for the arrival of a new baby. We wanted to avoid the dreaded effects of sibling rivalry. We read the *Berenstain Bears New Baby* book a dozen times. We did everything imaginable to make him feel that our new baby was also going to be his new baby. As mom's tummy began to grow, Anthony kept a little doll tucked beneath the front of his T-shirt.

Leah's birth fascinated Anthony. He was so excited. Nearly everyone who brought a present for Leah brought one for him. It was like Christmas in May. He loved his new sister, even though he noticed that she did not have any teeth. Everything was going just as we had planned.

On Leah's sixth day home, it happened. Anthony hopped out of the bathtub. His rosy skin smelled like soap and baby powder. He asked if he could have an apple. I said sure. He reappeared a few moments later. He placed one hand on the back of my chair while holding the apple in the other.

"Dad, I think I'm in trouble."

"What for?" I asked.

"Well, when I was getting my apple, I accidentally 'peed' in the refrigerator."

"You're right," I said. "You are in trouble."

What We Want

My children create many challenging situations. Occasionally, I am amused. Often, I feel frustrated and discouraged. Sometimes, I feel embarrassed and guilty. Our children are a measure of our success and worthiness. We judge ourselves by their success and achievements. We compare ourselves to other parents. We compare our children to other children. Have you ever watched people buy apples? We rotate each apple looking for a blemish. We hold it up to the light, examining the reflection. We squeeze each one for firmness. We study each competitor looking for the perfect apple.

Parents want perfect apples. We want successful children. We want them to be happy and well adjusted. We want them to feel good about themselves. We want children who are loving and respectful of others. We want them to be well behaved and self-motivated. We want them to be independent — not still living with us when they are thirty. All parents have the same goals and aspirations.

What We Have

Most parents confront the same behavior problems. We become annoyed repeating everything three times. We spend too much time arguing. We become drained from the nagging and whining and manipulating and quarreling. We become exhausted from shouting and threatening. At times, it seems that all we do is punish. We feel guilty for getting angry, but it appears to be the only way to get results. We blame ourselves and feel ineffective for not knowing what to do. There are times when we dislike our children because their misbehavior makes us feel so inadequate and miserable.

Raising well-behaved children is not easy. Many parents fail. Not because they are inadequate. Not because they lack love for their children. Not because they want something less than the best for their children. Unsuccessful parents are inconsistent. They procrastinate. They give warnings but do not follow through. They say things they do not mean. They lack patience. They punish in anger. Unsuccessful parents attend to the negative rather than the positive. They criticize too much. Parents who have discipline problems do not plan. They do not realize that they can be part of the problem. Parents are part of the problem because of their *patterns of reaction.*

Parents usually react in one of two ways. Sometimes parents react passively. They give in to misbehavior because they do not feel like confronting the problem, at least not right now. You will learn why giving in makes misbehavior worse. Sometimes parents react with anger. You will also learn how reacting with anger makes misbehavior worse.

The way you react to your children's misbehavior affects future misbehavior. A certain amount of misbehavior is normal. My guess is that young children misbehave about 5% of the time. (Some days it feels like 50%!) Knowing how to react to this 5% is crucial. Reacting correctly and consistently can reduce misbehavior from 5% to less than 2%. Reacting incorrectly can increase misbehavior to 10% or more.

Knowing how to react is essential. Knowing how to prevent discipline problems is more important. You can escape many predicaments by setting up a few guidelines in advance. Successful parents believe in prevention and planning. They are more proactive than reactive. You will learn several strategies to help you be more proactive.

What We Need

What factors contribute to successful parenting? Successful parents and their children are partners in discipline. Successful parents know that discipline is a teaching process. Discipline is not just punishment. Successful parents understand that their behavior and emotions affect their children's behavior and emotions. Successful parents model responsibility. They focus their attention and energy on the positive aspects of their children's behavior. Successful parents emphasize cooperation, not control. Successful parents teach their children to think for themselves. They teach children self-control. Successful parents build self-esteem. They know that healthy self-esteem is the main ingredient children need to develop self-confidence and resiliency.

Successful parents learn from their children. They develop reaction patterns that reduce misbehavior. Successful parents are consistent. They say what they mean and mean what they say. They follow through. Successful parents stay calm when their button is being pushed. They use punishments that teach, not get even. Successful parents connect special activities with good behavior.

Successful parents anticipate problems. They have a game plan. They have proactive strategies for managing tantrums, disobedience, fighting, arguments and power struggles. Successful parents have plans that teach the value of completing chores, earning allowances, and doing homework.

Successful parents do not let misbehavior keep them from enjoying their children. Successful parents are strict but positive. They are serious about the importance of proper conduct, but they have a childlike sense of humor whenever it is needed. Successful parents know how to appreciate their children, even when they are misbehaving. Most importantly, successful parents are open to change.

How This Book Will Help

This book will make your life easier. This book teaches you how to get your children to listen the first time you ask them to do something. It teaches you how to be more consistent. It shows you how to get your children to behave without getting angry. It explains how to use incentives without bribing. It shows you how to use punishments that teach. It explains how to punish your children without feeling punished yourself. It teaches you how to correct your children without arguments and power struggles. It empowers you to handle teasing and tantrums. It will even tell you what to do when one of your children "pees" in the refrigerator.

If you already have well-behaved children, thank your higher power. This book will help you too. It will make you more conscious of the successful strategies you are currently using. This book will show you how to maintain good behavior and it will prepare you for any future problems.

One of the best sources of help for parents is other parents. I realized this after watching parents who have attended my parenting workshops. It's thrilling to see parents pick each other's brains for techniques. They find ideas that will stop Jonathan's tantrums or get Heather to do her homework or get the twins to stop fighting.

This book is a collection of ideas that I have learned from parents. Parents who were fatigued and confused. Parents drained from yelling. Parents who felt imprisoned by their children. Parents who walked through life on a treadmill. Parents whose hearts were empty. Parents who sometimes felt like giving up. Parents who discovered a better way.

All the examples in this book are true stories from actual parents with real problems. The ideas in this book are simple and practical. Everything is explained with down-to-earth language.

There are a number of theories about parent and child behavior. Most authors accept one theory. They try to convince you that their ideas work for every parent and every child. After trying this approach, I decided it was insufficient. Since every parent and child is unique, why not use a variety of methods? Use the best from every theory. This book provides hundreds of ideas. Not all of them will work all the time. You need to select the ideas that make sense to you.

How We Learn Parenting Behavior

We learned most of our parenting behavior from our parents. Have you ever said something to your children and then realized you heard these same words when you were a child. "Be careful or you'll break your neck." "Be quiet and eat." We parent the way we were parented. We discipline as we were disciplined. Most ideas that we learned from our parents are helpful. Some are not. We pick and choose from these methods. Things we like, we use. Things we do not like, we do not use.

We also learn by watching other parents for good ideas. We learn by talking with friends. We learn from their experiences. They learn from our experiences. We share techniques that work.

We also learn by trial and error. Much of what we do with our children is based on our best guess at the time. Some things work; some fail. This happens to us all. Every first-born child is a test for most parents. You begin using trial and error the moment you get home from the hospital. I remember feeling confused and helpless. The baby is crying. What does it mean? Hungry? Lonely? Wet? Too warm? Too cold? Trial and error also applies to discipline. If sending your child to bed early works once, you will probably use it again.

The beliefs that you already have about parenting and discipline are fine. Learning from your parents and friends and learning by trial and error is normal. Add judgment and common sense and you have the substance for a solid foundation. This book will build on that foundation.

Love Does Not Always Light the Way

Too many parents have the false belief that if they love their children as much as possible, misbehavior will someday improve. Love, warmth and affection are essential. They are fundamentals. You also need knowledge.

Imagine you needed an operation. As you were about to be put under the anesthetic, your physician whispered in your ear. "I want you to know that I am not a surgeon. I'm not a doctor at all. Please don't worry. My parents are both doctors. I have a lot of friends who are doctors. I've asked a lot of questions about surgery. Just relax! I have a lot of common sense and I love my patients very much." Would you let this person use a scalpel on you?

Parents need training just as professionals need training. Children need trained parents as much as they need loving parents. Training pulls together all the good ideas you already have. Training provides structure and direction. Training provides a framework. Training gives you confidence. You learn that what you are doing is right. More confidence means more self-control, less anger, less guilt and less frustration. More confidence means more respect from your children. Without confidence, many parents are afraid to correct or punish their children. Some worry that their children will not like them. Some are afraid they might harm their children emotionally. So they let their children misbehave.

It Wasn't Like That When I Was Growing Up

Why doesn't discipline work the way it did 20 or 30 years ago? Why don't the old fashioned methods work? Why is being a parent so demanding and confusing? Parenting is more difficult because childhood is more difficult. Children are under pressure. Pressure to make adult decisions with the experience and emotions of a child. Pressure from peers. Pressure from school. Pressure from the media. Pressure that seeps down from the pressures on the parents. Pressure on our children translates into problems for us.

There are several changes in our culture that have a tremendous impact on discipline and our roles as parents. Our economy has created financial tension in families. Parents come home stressed. Their fuse is short. The rising divorce rate affects all of our children. Today, there are schools where 4 out of 5 children have experienced divorce. Single parenting is stressful.

Twenty years ago, everyone in the same town or neighborhood had the same values and beliefs. No matter where you went to play, the rules were the same. Everyone's parents had the same expectations. This is no longer true. Every family has their own standards. Our children experience many versions of right and wrong. This is confusing to children.

How do these changes in our society affect the way you discipline your children? Why won't the old ways work today? The old ways were simple solutions for a society with simple problems. Today's problems are more complicated. They require refined solutions. Our children live in the future, not the past. We have to cope with the adversity of our times. If you want to be a successful parent, you have to know how to discipline today's children. Parents need training. Not because parents are incapable, but because parenting is no longer simple.

Three Successful Promises

There are three promises that every parent needs to make to become more successful. Promise to have courage to be open and accept new ideas. If what you are doing is working, stick with it. If not, then have the courage to try something new.

Promise to have patience — plenty of patience. If your child is twelve years old, he has had twelve years to develop his behavior patterns. Give your child time to change. This is where most parents fail. We have gone from one hour dry cleaning to one-hour photos to one hour eye glasses to 30 minute tune-ups. Microwave dinners, car phones and express lanes have conditioned us to expect instant gratification. Technology has taught us impatience. We believe that because we are trying a new idea, changes should take place overnight. A few days is not long enough to test a new idea. Some methods take weeks to show improvement. Be patient.

Promise to practice. Every parent must practice. Even me. My children do not care one bit that I am a school psychologist who teaches parenting classes. When I'm home, I'm Dad. I get tested just like you. I have to practice, too. If you are willing to read about new ideas but do not practice them, give this book to someone else and buy a magic wand.

Summary

Children learn good behavior. Children learn misbehavior. Behavior does not occur by magic. It is not inherited. A well-behaved child is not the result of luck. Be encouraged — if children learn behavior, then children can learn to change behavior. Parenting behavior is also learned. Good parenting skills do not appear suddenly and instinctively. You can learn to be a more successful parent.

This is a book about parent behavior. It teaches you to examine your own behavior and determine when you are part of the problem. It prepares you to support yourself when your children tell you they hate you. It shows you how to stay calm when your button is being pushed. This book enables you to build healthy self-esteem in your children. It explains how to teach your children to think for themselves and withstand peer pressure. This book teaches you how to enjoy being a parent.

If you are in pursuit of well-behaved, well-adjusted children, you need to understand how your behavior is connected with your child's behavior. That's what I hope to teach you in this book. I hope to teach you how to behave so your children will, too!

Changing Your Behavior: Where to Begin

As you read the ideas in this book, you may think, "Sounds great. That will really work for me." Reading about a new technique is not the same as practicing a new technique. Practicing a new idea means changing your behavior. Any change in behavior means changing habits. Habits are not easy to change. Old habits are comfortable, new ones are not.

As you continue with this book, you will be learning about successful parent behaviors. You will be reading about strategies and techniques that you need to use more. You will learn about parent behaviors that are counter-productive. You will need to practice doing these behaviors less. You will also find that many of your present ideas are appropriate and need no change. As you read, make a list of behaviors that you need to practice more, behaviors you need to practice less, and behaviors that are appropriate and should be continued.

Since it takes about a month to develop new habits, review your list two or three times a week for the next four weeks. This review will help you solidify your new habits more quickly.

Behaviors I need to do *more*.

_____

_____

_____

_____

Behaviors I need to do *less*.

_____

_____

_____

_____

Behaviors that are appropriate and I need to *continue*.

_____

_____

_____

_____

Chapter 2

Redefining Discipline

"How do you discipline your children?"
"I scream a lot."
"Does that work?"
"Not usually. They might settle down for a
  few minutes."
"Then what?"
"They start fighting again."
"What do you do then?"
"I get mad and give each of them a spank-
  ing."
"Does that stop them?"
"For a little while."

When I ask parents how they discipline their children, most parents tell me how they punish their children.
They yell, scold, spank, take privileges away and restrict
their children to their bedrooms. Discipline and punishment are not the same. When used correctly, punishment
is a small part of the total discipline process.

Discipline includes all those things that we do as
parents to teach our children how to make better decisions. Discipline is teaching children how to make better
choices about their behavior. Discipline is teaching children to be responsible. Discipline is teaching children to
think for themselves. Discipline is teaching children that
they have the power to choose how they behave. These
definitions are completely different from the belief that
discipline is punishment. *Discipline means teaching decision-making*.

Emphasize Cooperation, Not Control

Many parents are confused about the purpose of discipline. They believe the purpose of discipline is to control a child's behavior — make him behave no matter what. This goal is unreasonable and unattainable. The purpose of discipline is not control. The purpose of discipline is cooperation. Cooperation means that your children choose to behave because it makes sense to behave. It feels good to behave. This is the goal of good discipline. Unfortunately, many parents spend hours each day chasing their children around the house trying to make them behave.

Discipline should not be a negative force that brings bad feelings to everyone involved. The thought of disciplining your children should not upset your stomach. I knew a father who became so angry with his children he began taking tranquilizers.

Imagine that your daughter makes a mess in the kitchen. The former view of discipline would cause you to think: "How should she be punished so she will not do it again?" You may get angry, yell or reprimand. You may spank her or send her to her room. Chances are that both of you end up feeling annoyed.

Discipline should provide your children with learning experiences. "What can I do so that she learns from this; so that she chooses not to do this again?" You want your daughter to clean up after herself. "Elena, I'm glad to see that you are old enough to make your own lunch. But I am disappointed that you left a mess. I know you can do better. Please go clean it up. Let me know if you need help."

There is an important difference between these two strategies. In the first scene, you are trying to control your child's behavior. The new approach encourages your child to control her own behavior. This strategy makes more sense. Seeking control is seldom a better tactic than seeking cooperation. Once you believe that discipline is teaching decision-making, you and your children will have an improved, cooperative attitude about discipline.

Are there ever circumstances when you should control your children? There are occasions, particularly with younger children, when you need to control. Your two-year-old daughter wants to play with an electrical wall outlet. You would control her by removing her from the situation. You decide for her. If you have a son who refuses to go somewhere with you, it is acceptable to take his hand and go. If your teenager drives carelessly, you would take away the car keys until he demonstrates safer habits.

The need for cooperation becomes more apparent as children grow older. You have less control over their behavior. You must rely on cooperation and trust. I once worked with a father who insisted that his fourteen-year-old son stay in the house after dinner. The opposition and resistance between father and son grew to the point of hatred. Dad installed a $2,200.00 burglar alarm to keep his son from going out the bedroom window. Installing the alarm was the father's last, desperate attempt at control. All it did was challenge the boy. It took the son four days to figure out how to deactivate the alarm.

Attempts to control teenagers are futile. You must depend on your teenagers to cooperate with your ideas of right and wrong. You must count on them to make their own decisions. Teenagers need to think for themselves, so when they face a strenuous choice, they will say, "Is this good for me?" Think of it this way. If your teenage daughter chooses to have sex, will she ask your permission? If your adolescent son decides to try pot, will he ask you first? Not likely.

How To Give Children Choices

Some parents make too many decisions for their children. They want to protect their children from making a wrong choice. They want to safeguard them against painful outcomes. This is understandable, but it denies your child opportunities to learn. It may give your child the message that he is incapable of making his own decisions. Use judgment and caution without being overprotective. Think about your child's choices, rules and activities in three ways. Some things are required: earning passing grades, working around the house. Some things you will negotiate: curfew, TV programs, make-up, snacks. Give them full authority in some choices: sports, music, school activities. As children mature and show more responsibility, gradually allow them more authority over their lives. If you expect more responsibility from your older children, give them more privileges. "You are three years older, I expect more from you." Higher expectations need a higher incentive. Allow older children a later bedtime, more allowance, more activities. This encourages them to continue to behave responsibly and make good decisions. It gives them confidence. They see you are a fair person. They will trust you. There is more specific information about this in Chapter 25.

Summary

Discipline is teaching children to make decisions. The purpose of discipline is teaching children to be cooperative. Begin emphasizing cooperation and responsible decision making at an early age. Have faith in your child's willingness to cooperate.

Children are either in control or under control. Discipline means teaching children to control themselves. If you want your children to be responsible decision-makers, you must teach them self-control. If you force control, they do not learn to master being *in* control. They do not develop self-control skills and habits. This results in children being out of control.

Part II: HOW CHILDREN LEARN
THEIR BEHAVIOR

Chapter 3

How Children Model

Children learn by copying. A child's potential to observe and imitate is a remarkable quality. Scientists refer to this as modeling. Children learn to speak by modeling. They learn language simply by listening, observing and imitating. Children learn attitudes, values, personal preferences, and even some habits by modeling.

Since children copy the behavior of the people around them, you have a powerful influence on your children's learning. Think carefully about your behavior. What you say and do in front of your children influences their thinking and behavior. You are their model.

Anthony was five. He and I went Christmas shopping. The parking lot was jammed. We drove around for several minutes looking for a place to park. I am not blessed with patience in these situations. Finally, I spotted a car pulling out. I drove up and put on my signal, indicating my intent. As the car backed out, another car sneaked ahead of me. I got so angry. I rolled my window down and yelled something obscene at the driver. We exchanged a few angry looks and then I continued my search for another parking place.

About twenty minutes later, Anthony and I were walking in the mall. I had cooled off. We were discussing what presents to buy. Without warning, he looked up and asked, "By the way Dad, what is an a-- h--- anyway?"

It felt like I was hit with a brick. What a shocking insight. He clearly heard me use bad language and he remembered exactly what I said. I was so embarrassed. I explained that it was not a nice word and I was wrong for saying it. I admitted that I was angry and frustrated because I could not find a parking place, I added that I hoped he would not use the word as I did. It was a moment of truth for me.

You can be a good example to your children 95% of the time. Isn't it fascinating how children always seem to catch you when you mess up? When children catch parents misbehaving, many parents get defensive. "Never mind what that word means. Don't ever let me hear you say it." This response is wrong. It closes communication. It tells your child that you can say bad words but he can not. The first thing your child will do when he gets to school the next day is start asking all his classmates what the word means.

How to be a Good Model

Do not get defensive when your child catches you misbehaving. Take advantage of this situation. Turn your discomfort into a valuable learning opportunity. When I was caught using a bad word, I explained that I was wrong. I made a mistake. I was angry. I took responsibility for my anger. I did not blame the person who took the parking place. I admitted my error. I apologized. What am I modeling now? Parents make mistakes. When I do, I admit it. I take responsibility. I apologize. These are invaluable qualities to model for your children.

Children learn from everything you do. If you lie about your twelve-year-old's age to avoid the extra price of an adult ticket, you teach your child that lying is okay. If you tell the person on the phone that your husband is not home, when he is, you teach your children that lying is okay. If you eat junk food, you teach your children to eat junk food. If you watch TV all day, you teach your children to watch TV all day. If you argue, yell or call people names, you teach your children these things. If you get angry at your children, you can expect them to get angry at others. If you yell something obscene at someone who takes your parking place, you teach your children to use obscene language.

When you speak in a calm voice instead of an angry one, you teach your children how to stay calm when provoked. When you apologize for using bad language you teach your children to take responsibility for mistakes. When you take responsibility for your anger, you teach your children to take responsibility for their anger. When you use polite language, you teach your children to be polite. When you share, you teach your children to share. When you are kind to others, you teach your children kindness. When you do your best, you teach your children to do their best. When you read a book, you teach your children proper attitudes about reading. When you eat healthful foods and exercise, you teach your children to eat healthful foods and exercise. When you behave in a responsible manner, you teach your children to behave in a responsible manner.

A horrible example of the effects of modeling is the epidemic of child abuse. Often, parents who are abusers were abused as children. When a violent and angry parent beats a child, the child learns that this is the way parents treat their children. When that child grows up, he will often treat his children the same way.

If your child's behavior concerns you, look closely at your behavior. Children learn what they live. When they live with responsible parents, they become responsible children. They will grow up to be responsible parents to your grandchildren. You have an obligation to be the best model that you can be. Always. Your children do as you do.

Children Learn From Their Surroundings

A second way that children learn is by experiencing things in their surroundings. Your child's surroundings contain you and other family members, playmates, people in the neighborhood, classmates, teachers, the lunchroom, the playground, TV, movies, books, magazines, music, etc. These are the ingredients in your child's environment — the world that surrounds him. Learning by experience is different than copying. If a child touches hot food, he learns that hot food hurts fingers. The child learns about hot food through experience, not by modeling.

Children behave to fit into their environment. If the environment rewards playing with dolls, children play with dolls. If the environment rewards playing soccer, children play soccer. If the environment rewards belonging to a gang, children join gangs.

The environment shapes your child's learning and behavior. Parents who value education have children who do well in school. Families that encourage teamwork have cooperative, hard-working children. Neighborhoods that foster harmony have children who play together nicely.

Summary

Your children copy what you say and do. They learn many of their behaviors from you. Be a good example. Your children learn from their surroundings. Provide experiences that teach your values and encourage self-discipline and responsibility. The remainder of this book teaches you how to be a good model and how to create a positive learning environment for your children.

Chapter 4

You And Your Children Learn From Each Other

Every time four-year-old Michael goes to the supermarket with his mother, Connie, he asks for a candy bar. Connie says, "No." A few minutes later, Michael begins pleading for a candy bar. Connie still says "No." By the third aisle, Michael is starting a tantrum. His begging escalates into demanding. Connie still says "No." His face gets red. He kicks his feet and shakes the shopping cart. Connie threatens to spank him if he does not stop. He doesn't. Aisle 5 — Michael's tantrum explodes. Connie looks for a place to hide, but she is in frozen foods. Tears! Screams! Kicking and shaking. Everyone is staring. Connie can take no more. She gives in. She buys the candy bar.

Connie has taught Michael three things. She has taught him that the word No is meaningless. Connie's responses were, No, No, No, No, Yes. That means that when Connie says No she does not mean No. She means ask again and again, and get more demanding each time. When your behavior becomes so obnoxious that I cannot stand it any more, I will change my No to Yes. It's like magic! No becomes Yes! Connie has taught Michael to be persistent in a negative way.

Connie has taught Michael how to have tantrums. She has not done this on purpose, but she has done it. She has taught Michael that screaming and demanding pays off. If you scream and yell loud enough and long enough you can get a candy bar. A candy bar is Michael's reward for having a tantrum. Have a tantrum — get a candy bar. Have a tantrum — get your way.

Connie has taught Michael that she does not mean what she says. She makes threats but does not follow through. She told him to be quiet or she would spank him. What did she do instead? She bought him a candy bar. Here is what Michael might be thinking. "Well I got my Snickers on aisle 7 this week. Last week it was aisle 8. I'm doing better. I love it when Mom gives me the 'quiet or I'll spank you' routine. That had me worried the first time I heard it. That was two years ago and she hasn't followed through yet. Maybe next week I'll try for aisle 5."

Michael has taught Connie a few things, too. He has taught her how to gain peace and quiet and stop the embarrassment. Buy the candy bar. All of Connie's other attempts at quieting Michael were futile. She could only achieve peace with candy. This has happened before. A pattern has been established. It will happen again. Giving in to Michael's demands is the only way to have peace and quiet.

There are parents who live every day of their lives this way. They believe that giving in to demands is the only way to stop the tantrum. *This is a big mistake.* Reward a child's tantrum once, and you will be teaching your child to have more tantrums in the future. Give in to your child's shouted demands once, and you will be listening to shouted demands again and again.

What can you do if you are already trapped in this dilemma? Here is a plan that quieted the supermarket battleground. Connie stopped taking Michael on long shopping trips. She began by taking him on short trips to the local convenience store. Before they left the house, Connie would explain how she wanted Michael to behave. Connie would explain where they were going and what they were going to buy. She would show Michael the shopping list with three or four items on the list. At the bottom of the list, Connie would write a treat, such as cookies. She would often ask Michael what he wanted to put on the list. She would let Michael hold the list while they shopped. This gave Michael ownership in shopping. It gave him something to do. It gave him something to control. As they obtained each item, he would cross the item off the list. If Michael did a good job, he could choose the cookies.

"Michael, you and I are going shopping. I want you to listen to me while we are at the store. I do not want any teasing. You can help me by holding the shopping list. You can cross out the items as we put them in the basket. If you do as I ask and do not tease, you can pick out the cookies. I know you can do it."

I explained to Connie that while they were shopping, she would need to be generous with encouragement. "You are doing a good job of keeping track of the list. Thank you." "You are waiting nicely. Thank you, Michael." "I appreciate your help." After two weeks of practice and a few minor setbacks, the plan proved to be working.

As Connie and Michael became more familiar with the rules of shopping, they took their plan back to the supermarket. Connie began with quick trips and short lists. This strategy eased the transition from the convenience store to the supermarket. Gradually, she was able to extend her shopping time. Michael had learned how to behave. So had Connie.

Here is an example of a child who does not listen. Brad is an active and curious twelve-year-old. Most of the time, Brad's behavior is fine. About once or twice a day, Brad becomes a little too excited, active and loud. His father, Richard, always begins by calmly and politely asking Brad to settle down and play more quietly. Brad always responds to this initial request the same way. He ignores Dad completely. The next round occurs a while later. Richard raises his voice. "Quiet down or you will go to your room!" Brad responds, "Okay, Dad." Brad makes no real effort to be quiet. Finally, Richard becomes angry and starts yelling. "If you do not get quiet right now I am getting out the paddle." This time, Brad becomes quiet and remains so for several hours.

Let's examine what Richard and Brad have learned from each other. Brad might say, "I've learned that I do not have to do what Dad asks the first time. I don't even have to do much when he raises his voice the first time. I do not have to do anything until he starts talking about the paddle. Then he is serious."

Richard might be thinking that Brad is a child who just does not listen. This is partly true. Dad is also part of the problem. If Richard would admit this, his analysis of the situation would expand. "One thing I have learned is that my threats do not work. Anger and the paddle get results. Calm and polite requests do not. I have to do something else. I have to change the way I am handling this. I have to figure out how to get Brad to listen without always having to get out the paddle."

Richard has reached an important insight here. He realized that the way in which he reacts to Brad is part of the reason that Brad does not listen. Many parents do not like to admit this. It is easier to justify misbehavior as a phase. Many parents cannot face the idea that they might be doing something wrong. In most situations, both you and your children need a behavior change.

There is another lesson in this example. Whenever you use punishment alone to control a misbehavior, you will get a recycling pattern of the misbehavior. Richard threatens Brad a few times. Brad doesn't listen. Richard becomes angry and gets out the paddle. Brad become quiet. *For a while!* Sooner or later, Brad will start up again. It may be in an hour or two, or the next day, but his misbehavior will return. Why? Because this next time he may get away with it a little more than last time. Brad gets loud. Richard threatens. Brad doesn't listen. Richard gets angry. The cycle continues.

Richard needs to be consistent. He needs to follow through the first time he asks Brad to be more quiet. He needs to follow Brad's refusal to play more quietly with a consequence, such as taking away the stereo or some other privilege.

Here is an example of cooperation. Mrs. Harmon and eleven-year-old Jane have an agreement. For every 30 minutes that Jane studies or reads a book, she may watch 30 minutes of television. The agreement has been written down. Mrs. Harmon has found no need to nag or argue with Jane. Jane clearly understands her part of the bargain. What have mother and daughter learned from this arrangement? They have learned to cooperate. Mrs. Harmon has found a way to get Jane to read. Jane has found a way to earn TV time.

This type of agreement is called a contract. Children learn what you expect from them. Children learn what they can expect from you. Written contracts are useful tools for teaching responsibility, especially with teenagers. You will learn more about contracts in Chapter 7.

What's the Pay-Off?

These examples demonstrate that parents and children learn from each other. How does the learning actually happen? In all three examples, the principles of learning are the same. Learning occurs because of a pay-off. We behave to earn a pay-off. We do things to get what we want. Let's examine the behaviors and the pay-offs in each example.

Michael's behavior was a tantrum. Michael's pay-offs were the candy bar and winning over mom, — power and control. Connie's behaviors were giving in and buying the candy bar. Connie's pay-offs were a few minutes of peace and no further embarrassment. They each got what they wanted. What's wrong? The method. Michael got what he wanted by screaming in public. Connie got what she wanted by giving her authority and control to her child. Michael is only four. If Michael is demanding at four, he will likely be incorrigible at fourteen.

Brad's behavior was ignoring Richard's requests. Brad's pay-off was having his way a little longer. At first, Richard's behavior was to threaten and do nothing. Once he was angry, Richard's behavior was to get the paddle. His pay-off was that Brad finally became quiet. The paddle has some immediate pay-off. It is not effective in the long run. Brad is not learning to be quiet. He is not learning to cooperate. He is learning that he only has to become quiet when Dad brings out the paddle. If Brad is like most children, he will become noisy again. Dad will go through his threats again. The cycle may never end.

Jane's behavior was spending time doing homework and reading. She has learned cooperation and self-control. Her pay-off was more TV time. Mrs. Harmon's behavior was allowing Jane more TV time because Jane was making good decisions about homework. Mrs. Harmon has learned to negotiate and plan. Mrs. Harmon's pay-off was that Jane is studying and reading more. Not only do both parent and child get what they want, the method for getting what they want is constructive rather than destructive.

How to Redirect Misbehavior

If your child misbehaves frequently, it means that he has not learned appropriate methods of getting what he wants. Think about your child's pay-off. What does your child hope to gain by this misbehavior? Figure out the pay-off and then do not give in. Do not reward unacceptable behavior. Teach him to redirect his behavior. Give him an appropriate alternative that will enable him to earn his pay-off. If he seeks attention, show him how to get your attention without misbehaving. "Matthew, I will not give in to teasing. If you want me to read you a story, you need to stop whining. Please go sit for few minutes. Then come back and ask me in a polite voice." Teach him there are acceptable ways of getting what he wants. This takes time, commitment and planning.

Connie stopped giving-in to Michael's shouted demands. She taught him how to get what he wanted through proper behavior. Help with shopping, stay calm, have a little patience, and you can earn a little treat. Everyone is happy and mother has remained in charge of the situation, not the child.

Your Turn

Kyle has an answer for everything. No matter what Debbie asks him to do, he argues. "Kyle, would you please take the trash out to the garage?" Kyle frowns and acts annoyed. "I'll do it later. Why do I have to do it now. Can't somebody else do something for a change?" Debbie is not sure what to do. She tries to explain why Kyle should do what she asks. She tries to stay calm but ends up getting angry and frustrated. When she does, Kyle gets worse. He becomes angry and hostile. He screams and yells and has a tantrum. Debbie cannot take these outbursts. After a few minutes of fighting and arguing, Debbie gives up.

She takes out the trash herself. Kyle pouts for a few more minutes and then returns to normal. What is Kyle's pay-off for arguing? What is Debbie's pay-off for giving in? Write down your answers before reading further. For now, just think about the pay-offs. You will read about solutions in the next chapter.

Summary

We make decisions about our behavior to get what we want. Sometimes we want things. Sometimes we want our way. We avoid behaviors that might cause us to lose things or make us feel uncomfortable.

Kyle's pay-off was getting his way. He argued to avoid doing what his mother asks. Debbie's pay-off was putting an end to the battle. She got peace and quiet.

Understanding pay-offs enables you to make changes in the way you discipline your children. Think about your child's pay-off for misbehavior. Does he get his way? Does he succeed in getting you angry and upset? Does he get to avoid doing what you ask? Once you identify your child's pay-off, you have your first new discipline tool. Then determine your pay-off. What makes you react the way you do? Do you give in to avoid a hassle? Are you afraid of what your child might do if you do not give in?

If you want your children's behavior to change, look at your own behavior. This is an uncomfortable experience for me. It may also be uncomfortable for you. Try not to feel threatened or defensive. Make a commitment to change yourself first. Your change in behavior affects your children's change in behavior. The way that you behave toward your children affects the way they behave toward you and everyone else. There is a good title for a book somewhere in there.

Part III: HOW TO FOCUS ON THE
POSITIVE BEHAVIORS AND ATTITUDES
IN YOUR CHILDREN

Chapter 5

Spotlight Good Behavior

Joey decides to stop associating with Tim. He has decided that Tim gets in too much trouble. Joey's parents praise his decision. "That took a lot of courage. It shows you are thinking for yourself. Growing up isn't always easy. You seem to be handling it quite well. We are proud of you. We hope you are proud of yourself."

Tiffany runs up to her mother. "My room is clean, mom. Come and take a look." Mom examines the room. "Great job, Tiffany. You should be proud of yourself. Your room looks very neat."

Joey's parents and Tiffany's mom are using positive feedback. They are looking for good decisions. They are pointing out the things their children are doing well. It is like shining a spotlight on good behavior.

Positive feedback is the most powerful tool you have to improve your children's behavior and self-esteem. Positive feedback is a pay-off for good behavior. Positive feedback means using praise or incentives to encourage good decision-making. Positive feedback is not something new, but we often forget to use it. If you desire better behavior from your children, increasing your awareness and use of positive feedback is essential.

How to Use Positive Feedback

You can use positive feedback in two ways — to increase desirable behavior or decrease undesirable behavior. Using positive feedback to strengthen a desired behavior is easy. Simply look for a good behavior. When it occurs, reinforce it. When your children are well behaved, reward them with a few words of praise or encouragement, a hug, or a privilege.

You would like your children to share with each other. When your children share something, reinforce the sharing. You could say: "I like the way you are sharing." "I see you have decided to share your toys this morning. That's a good decision." "I am proud of the way you are sharing the TV. That shows you are growing up. Good for you!"

Positive feedback is simple to use. The difficult part is remembering to look for the good behavior. Often, we only see the misbehavior in our children and take good behavior for granted. Be proactive. Strengthen good behavior by telling your children you appreciate it. Focus on the positive aspects of your children's behavior. That takes practice. If you increase your use of positive feedback and make no other changes in your parenting behavior, your children will start making better decisions.

Replacement

You can also use positive feedback to eliminate or weaken a misbehavior. This technique works with patterns of misbehavior. Not misbehavior that is staring you in the face. First, determine the misbehavior. Next, determine the opposite behavior. Six-year-old Nathan argues and fights with his four-year-old sister, Ashley. The opposite of this misbehavior occurs when Nathan is playing nicely and cooperating with Ashley. Praise Nathan for playing nicely. Playing cooperatively will *replace* fighting. He will learn a more acceptable way of playing. "You are helping your sister draw. Good for you." The arguing and fighting will occur less often. This is a simple but effective strategy. Use positive feedback to strengthen the opposite behavior. The original misbehavior will decrease.

I have been convinced of the power of positive feedback for most of my professional life. For the past twenty years, I have been working extensively with school programs for behavior disordered children. These programs would often take children who were unable to function in a regular school program because of disruptive behavior. Many of these children were seriously emotionally disturbed, many were delinquent, and many were undisciplined. Regardless of the severity of their problems, nearly every child made improvements within the first week. People who knew these children's history were amazed. How did these children improve their behavior so quickly? The staff would pile the positive feedback so deep the children needed a periscope. The staff stopped looking for negative behavior. They looked for the positive.

Most parents see the value in using positive feedback. It is common sense. There are some who resist the use of rewards and incentives. Whenever I face this concern, I explain how children are motivated. Many children are self-motivated to be well behaved and cooperative. This is not the case with all children. Positive feedback gives children a motivation boost. It builds self-esteem. Positive feedback encourages children to be more self-motivated.

Adults need positive feedback, too. Paychecks are an example of positive feedback. Your self-motivation would not keep you at work if you were not paid. This is how our society operates. The sooner children learn this the better. Parents who object to using rewards must remember that their goal is to have children who make good decisions. Not all children are self-motivated to achieve this goal. Using positive feedback gets things going in the right direction. Then self-motivation takes over.

Aim for Self Reward

Use positive feedback that teaches your child to value himself. "You made the right choice because you knew it was the correct thing to do." It is all right for children to behave and work hard to please their parents. It is better when they behave and work hard for themselves.

"I like the way you did that." (Good)
"Well done. You should be proud of yourself." (Better)

The second statement creates a sense of success and self-value. It is aimed at building self-esteem. Whenever you reward your child with an incentive, such as an allowance, be sure to add a comment that causes your child to think about doing the right thing. "You did a wonderful job on your chores. Here's your allowance. I hope you feel good about yourself."

Children Believe What You Tell Them

Children act the way you expect them to act. If you tell your son that he is noisy, he will live up to that expectation. If you tell your son that he knows how to play quietly, he will live up to that expectation. When you put a T-shirt on a child that says "Here Comes Trouble," you are encouraging your child to think of himself as a trouble maker. Here is what many parents say to teenagers who have messy bedrooms.

"I do not understand why you're so
sloppy. Look at this mess. What's wrong

with you? You can't even keep your closet straight. Aren't you ashamed? When was the last time you made this bed? You'll never change."

What is the parent saying? You are a slob. That's why your room is a mess. You will always be a slob. That's what I expect from you. I am giving up hope of any improvement. Here is the same teenager, same bedroom, different message.

"You know Zack, this is not like you. You are a neater person than this. I know you can be tidy. I know you have pride in yourself. I'm sure you can do better in the future. Don't you think so, too?"

Here is what the parent is saying. I trust you. I have confidence in you. You can do better. Do it for your own sake. Your child will not make radical changes overnight, but you will be planting a healthier seed in his mind.

Be specific when you praise your children. Praise the behavior, not your child. "Your room looks great. It looks like you worked hard. I hope you are proud." Do not say, "You are such a good boy for cleaning your room." This has a double message. Is your son not good when his room is unkempt? Be generous with praise and encouragement, but use it wisely. Undeserved praise can lead to conceit or false confidence. Do not tell your child he has worked hard if he has not.

By praising specific behavior, you clearly indicate correct decision making. You call attention to strengths. This gives your child confidence. He will feel capable of making good decisions.

Children need encouragement, especially children with poor self-esteem and children who lack persistence and determination. Encouragement gives children a boost of motivation. It helps them through difficult situations. It helps them face fears and withstand stress. It helps them solve problems and feel successful. Encouragement provides support, trust and belief.

Tell your child that you love and value him. Accept your child for what he is, not for what he does. Show trust and confidence in your child's abilities and decisions. Recognize effort and improvement.

How to Use Encouragement

How to show trust:
> "I like the way you handled that."
> "Knowing you, I am sure you will do fine."
> "I think you can do it."
> "I am sure you can decide this by yourself.
> If you need help, I'll be right here."
> "I would like to know your opinion about
> ...."

How to show the importance of hard work:
> "If you keep working, you'll probably get
> it."
> "Working hard pays off."
> "Hard work is not always easy, but it's al-
> ways worth it."

How to point out strengths and improvements:
> "It looks as if you worked hard at ...."
> "Look at the progress you have made in ...."
> "You have really improved in ...."

How to teach children to learn from mistakes:
> "So you made a mistake, what can you do
> about it?"
> "If you are not satisfied, what can you do?"

How to encourage responsibility:
> "It's up to you."
> "If you want to."
> "You can decide that for yourself."
> "Your decision will be fine with me."

Your Turn

Patty usually puts off doing her homework until the last possible minute. Today, she comes home from school and announces, "I have a lot of homework. I am going to get started before dinner." How can mother spotlight this decision?

Remember Kyle and Debbie? Kyle argues about everything his Mom asks him to do. Debbie often argues in return. In most cases, she gives in. Kyle wins. How can Debbie use positive feedback to help neutralize Kyle's constant arguing?

Summary

Positive feedback encourages your children to make good decisions. When Patty started her homework, she made a mature decision. It would be easy to miss what Patty is doing. "It's about time she started growing up a little." This would be a mistake. Do not let Patty's effort go unnoticed. "Patty, I am glad to see you get started on your homework. You will be happy with yourself when you are finished. You will have the rest of the evening free. It seems like a good decision to me."

Use positive feedback to reduce misbehavior. Even children like Kyle sometimes do what they are asked without an argument. Debbie needs to look for cooperation. "Kyle, thanks for helping me fold the laundry. I appreciate your help. I really appreciate the fact you didn't argue about it." By calling attention to the times when Kyle does not argue, Debbie is emphasizing his good behavior. This will encourage more cooperation from Kyle in the future.

Children believe what you tell them. Children act the way you expect them to act. If you focus on positive qualities you will build stronger positive qualities. Use praise and encouragement that teaches your children to value themselves.

I once saw a poster with a child looking rather discouraged. The caption read, "When I mess up, no one forgets. When I do well, no one sees." Positive feedback is easy to use, but we often forget. Retrain yourself to look for the positive qualities in your children. Look for good decisions. Spotlight good behavior.

Chapter 6

Never Give Away The Ice Cream

Wise parents connect special activities to good behavior. About ten years ago, I was spending a few days with some friends from high school. They have three children of various ages. One evening, we all piled into their van and went out for ice cream. Later that night, after the children had all gone to bed, we began talking about being parents. Albert asked if I had any suggestions. I said, "Never give away the ice cream."

I explained that at no time was any connection made between their children's behavior that day and our trip for ice cream. Successful parents connect special events to good behavior. "You have had an excellent day today. Mom and I would like to take you out for some ice cream." You can be more specific: "I saw you sharing several times today. That's something that makes Mom and me feel fantastic. When we feel good, we feel like doing something special."

I am not suggesting that we stuff sweets in our children's mouths whenever they are well behaved. I advise most parents to avoid sweets in favor of special activities. There are many ways to make the connection between having a good day and special events; going out for dinner, going to a movie, or even going for a Sunday afternoon drive. What about days when behavior has not been so good? Do not go out for ice cream on bad days.

Do not give special activities away. I have always found that teachers who are good disciplinarians use this idea instinctively. These teachers make statements such as, "Danny, you worked hard on math this morning. Please take this note to the office for me." "Jillian, you really helped Jason with his reading, please help me hand out these papers." I once observed a teacher who said, "Beth, you have been pleasant to work with this afternoon. I'd like you to stay at the end of the line and shut the lights off when we go to Art class." This clever teacher made a privilege out of being last in line.

Activity Incentives

Activity incentives are things children want to do. Playing video games, talking on the telephone and going out with friends are examples of activity reinforcers. Use activity incentives this way: first you work, then you play. Clean your room before you play video games. Do your homework before you watch television. Do not get trapped by promises. "I will study after the movie."

Always add an encouraging comment when your child earns an activity. "I hope you feel good about earning extra TV time." Emphasize feeling good about yourself, not the TV time. Enhance activities by becoming involved. Playing a game is fun. Playing a game with a parent is more fun.

There are special privilege activities such as staying up late or spending the night at a friend's home. A few years ago, we were celebrating Father's Day by going to a movie. "When is Brother's Day?" asked Anthony. "There is Mother's Day and Father's Day, why not Brother's Day?" We now have a surprise Brother's Day and Sister's Day each year. We do something special for each child.

Connect privileges to good behavior — but be careful. Do not dangle every little activity in front of your children's noses. That will give them the wrong idea. You do not want them to think they have to be perfect. They will resent you for this and develop a poor attitude about working toward goals. Allow some fun activities to happen routinely. You also do not want them to think that every time they behave, you have to come up with a special reward. Children need to learn that good behavior is important because it is the right thing to do.

Tangible Incentives

Tangible incentives are things children want. Examples are food, toys, CD's, money, etc. Always accompany tangible incentives with words of thanks and encouragement. "Here's your allowance Sue. You did a great job on your chores this week. Good for you."

What follows is a list of incentives. This list was developed with the help of more than three thousand parents over a five year period. Whenever I taught a class, I would have parents write down examples of incentives that worked with their children. I collected their ideas and compiled this list. You can use ideas from this list to create a menu of incentives. This menu can be used with charts and contracts, which are discussed in the next chapter.

Summary

Connect special activities to good behavior. This will teach your children that good behavior is worthwhile. When you use an activity or tangible incentives, always add a few words of thanks and encouragement. Spotlight the good behavior, not the specific incentive.

Incentives for Children Who are Under Twelve Years Old

Hugs and kisses/Praise and encouragement
Complimenting your child in front of others
Using the computer
One-on-one time with a parent
Brother's Day/Sister's Day
A special day with a parent
Roughhousing with a parent
Surprises
Back rubs
Thank you notes in the lunch box
Thank you notes through the mail
Having lunch at school
Books/Reading a story
Posters
Science kits
Working on models, building kits
Gardening
Playing games/Board games/puzzles
Magic tricks
Painting/drawing/supplies
Using a calculator
Playing outside/Playing catch
Sporting events
Baseball cards
Going for a walk/Going on a family bike ride
Going for a drive in the car
Going on a mystery ride
Sitting in the front seat
New clothes
Watching television
Using the VCR/renting a movie

Playing video games
Using the telephone
Marble jar
Making popcorn
Staying up late on weekends
Spending time at a friend's house
Spending the night at a friend's house
Having a friend come to the house
Having a slumber party
Making a blanket tent
Camp-out in the backyard
Singing songs/Playing music
Special trips
Going to a relative's house
Kite flying
Going swimming, fishing/skating, bowling
Playing miniature golf
Going to the movies
Going to the zoo, park, museum, library
Going out to eat
Allowing child to choose the restaurant
Having a pizza delivered
Bubble baths/toys in tub
Brushing hair
Helping prepare a meal/dessert
Helping clean up
Helping mom or dad with projects
Treats/Ice cream
Stickers/sticker books/happy faces
Stars/points on a chart
Money/allowance/savings account
Mystery jar with awards inside

Incentives for Children Twelve and Older
(Many of the items listed above)

Compliments
Activities with friends/Going to the Mall/Shopping
Computer time/On-line account
New clothes
Cosmetics/Hair Styled
Snacks
Money/allowance/Doing work for money
Having a weekly goal
Projects/hobby supplies
Having a friend over for lunch/dinner
Going out with a friend for lunch/dinner
Choosing an activity for the family
Time alone/Being allowed to do things alone/Choice time
Staying up later than younger siblings
Music/stereo time/Tapes, CD's
School materials
Pets/pet supplies
Special trips with school, church, clubs
Dances/Parties/Evening events/Dating
Telephone time/own phone line
Skateboarding
Sporting events
Playing cards
Driving lessons/Using the car/Chauffeur privileges
Working on cars/Using tools
Extended Curfew
Concerts
Cooking
Decorating their room
Pick their own time to do chores
Going on a business trip with parent

Chapter 7

Charts And Contracts

Solidify responsibility with a chart or contract. Charts are a picture of the agreement between you and your children. A contract is a written agreement between you and your children. Charts and contracts help you focus on goals. Charts and contracts help you keep records. They enable you to evaluate the behaviors that have improved and those that need further planning. Charts work best for children up to age twelve. Older children usually prefer contracts.

A Simple Chart

A posted chart becomes a visual reminder to be consistent. Charts prompt you to look for good behavior. They provide positive interactions between you and your children. They promote a healthy family climate. They encourage everyone to work together. Charts furnish both parents with an identical strategy. This increases consistency between parents.

Use a chart to reinforce good behavior. Identify the priority behaviors you want to increase. List each behavior on the chart. When your child behaves, put a smile face in the box. At the end of the day, add up the number of faces.

Points, check marks, plus signs or stickers work equally well. Awards on the chart are enough to satisfy some children. They do not always need other incentives. Some children need stronger incentives.

Trade smile faces for a reward or incentive. Each smile face could be worth a minute or two of extra story time, game time, or extra play time before going to bed. Some children like a reward each day plus a bonus activity for having a good week. Each smile face could be worth game time at the end of the day. Then total the smile faces for the week. Having a friend spend the night costs 15 smile faces. Be flexible. Do what works best.

Jenny's Chart
☺ = Two extra minutes of story time!

Behavior	Mon	Tues	Wed	Thur	Fri	Sat	Sun
Shares her toys	☺ ☺	☺ ☺ ☺	☺ ☺ ☺	☺ ☺ ☺ ☺	☺ ☺ ☺	☺ ☺ ☺	☺ ☺ ☺
Listens the first Time	☺ ☺ ☺ ☺	☺ ☺	☺ ☺ ☺	☺ ☺ ☺	☺ ☺ ☺ ☺	☺ ☺ ☺	☺ ☺ ☺

Daily Total   6   5   6   7   7   6   7
Weekly Total   44

Always accompany an incentive with an encouraging statement. It is important to earn an award. It is more important to develop a sense of responsibility. Aim for self reward. "You had a great week. I'm glad Trina can spend the night. I hope you feel proud of yourself."

Select behaviors that increase the chances of success. Do not load the chart with troublesome misbehaviors. Your child will perceive the chart as impossible. Choose some behaviors that are easy and fun. You can also change the behaviors. You may have a list of eight or more priority behaviors. Rotate two or three behaviors each week. This keeps things interesting.

Have a section for bonus points. Anytime your child does something extra helpful or kind, add a smile face. When you see special effort, add a smile face. Children respond favorably to this technique. You can use a chart to improve a child's attitude. Craig will talk politely to his sister. Each time that Craig is polite to his sister, catch him. Put a smile face on his chart. Tell him you appreciate his politeness.

Eventually, you want your children to work for a few days or a week before receiving a reward. You want your children to learn that rewards require hard work. Begin with rewards at the end of each day, then require two days, etc. I worked with a teacher who used charts. Her students could use points earned for good behavior to buy activities and prizes. After a few weeks, she decided her students needed to work a little harder. She taught a lesson on inflation and raised all the prices of the prizes.

Some parents provide their children with a menu of incentives. Each incentive costs a certain number of points. Renting a movie for the VCR might cost 10 points. Making popcorn costs 10 points. Having a friend over costs 15 points. This technique teaches children to save and budget their points. It also teaches them that good behavior and hard work are worth responsibility and freedom. Maintain high interest and motivation by changing the incentives. Every few weeks, add new items to the menu. Look at the incentives at the end of Chapter 6.

Develop charts for a week at a time. You may choose a five, six or seven day week. Some parents only use charts during the busy work week. Some parents use the chart seven days a week to provide a high level of consistency. Do what works. Some parents use laminated tagboard and an erasable marker. That way the chart can be reused each week. Some parents draw a grid on a sheet of paper and make several photocopies. Some parents create the chart on a computer. They can make changes and print a new version each week.

Develop charts with your children. Dual participation causes children to have ownership in the chart. Let your children draw designs and color the chart. Let them suggest some of the behaviors and incentives. Involvement creates interest and motivation.

Charts provide you with a vehicle for immediate reinforcement. You can use a chart to call attention to good behavior. When your child behaves, walk over and add a smile face. Charts tell your children what you expect from them and what they can expect from you. Charts encourage children to remember the rules. You can use charts to redirect a child who is beginning to misbehave.

> "Alex, I want you to see something be-
> fore you get into trouble. Look at your chart.
> Look how well you have been listening. Look
> how you have improved. I know you feel
> proud about yourself. I know you can make
> a better decision. I know you can behave."

Here is the wrong way. "I don't know why you can't behave for more than three days. This chart is supposed to make you behave."

Charts help you avoid arguments. Written expectations and consequences permit no leeway for misinterpretation. Your children can see what they have or have not done. Charts teach responsibility. Charts show children how they are doing. Charts give your child feedback about his behavior. When your child is doing well, a chart shows progress. This creates feelings of success and increases motivation. When your child is not doing well, a chart will show the exact behaviors he needs to improve. You and your child can concentrate on the behaviors that need work.

A Chart to Promote Effort in School

Some parents have used charts to improve school behavior. If your child's teacher asks you for assistance, have the teacher send you a note each day. If your child has a good day, he can earn extra smile faces. You can be more specific with school behaviors, such as: follow the school rules; finish all your work; and turn homework in on time.

Dana's Chart
* = 3 minutes of video games after homework

Behavior	Sun	Mon	Tue	Wed	Thur	Fri	Sat
Listens the first time	* * * * * *	* * * * * *	* * * **	* * * * *	* * ** * *	* * * * * *	* * ** * **
Speaks politely	* * * * * *	* * * ** * *	* * * * *	* * ** * *	* * * * * *	* * ** * *	* * ** * *
Had a good day in school	* ** * * *	* * * ** * *	* * * * * *	* * * * *	* * ** * **	* * * * * *	* * ** * **
Bonus Points	* * * ** *	* * * * *	* * ** *	* * * * * *	* * ** * ** *	* * ** * ** *	* * ** * **
Daily Total	24	26	21	22	27	26	27
Weekly Total	24	52	77	99	128	158	190

School points:
    1. Follow the school rules   = * * *
    2. Finish all your work   = * * *
    3. Homework in on time   = * * *

Dana's teacher sends a note home each day. Dana can receive up to 3 stars a day for each of the three behaviors listed on his note. Have your child's teacher award the stars at school. You post the stars on the chart at home.

Checklists

A chart can be used as a checklist. Use a checklist whenever you ask your child to do a task that has several parts. Checklists promote success. A checklist breaks a complex set of behaviors into bite size pieces. The task does not look so overwhelming to the child. Use a checklist for morning routine, bedtime routine, cleaning bedrooms or weekend chores.

Getting Myself Ready for Bed

	Mon	Tue	Wed	Thur	Fri
Put dirty clothes away	✓				
Brush my teeth	✓				
Take my bath	✓				
Go to the toilet	✓				
Read for 20 minutes	✓				

Checklists teach children accountability. Checklists teach children about the adult world. There are recurring events in our lives that are not always exciting and stimulating. We do these jobs to keep order in our lives. It is best to teach these responsibilities to children when they are young. A checklist may or may not earn other rewards. Some parents do not think it is wise to use rewards to teach children household duties. Other parents do use rewards. Use what works for your children.

Contracts

A contract is a written agreement between you and your child. A contract specifies what you expect from him and what he can expect from you. Contracts work well for teenagers. A contract can be used for the same objectives as charts: effort in school, a checklist of behaviors at home or chores and allowance. A contract can be very similar to a chart. I have worked with many teenagers whose contract looked like a chart in every way except the word *chart* was changed to *contract* at the top of the page. Contract sounds better. A contract can look like a chart or it can look like a real contract. (See the example on the next page.)

Be specific when you write a contract. Do not say, "Cortney will be good for two weeks." Clarify what "being good" actually means. Expectations that are clearly written can not be the subject of an argument. Develop a contract for one or two weeks at a time.

A contract teaches teenagers to be responsible. It gives them direction and incentive. They learn what to do and why it is important. Contracts motivate teenagers to make good choices. Contracts help them feel mature and important.

Charts and contracts enable your children to plan for long term goals. Suppose your child wants to earn a new outfit. The cost of a new outfit necessitates that your child may have to work for several weeks. Charting or contracting his behaviors and work around the house enables you and your child to monitor his progress toward his goal.

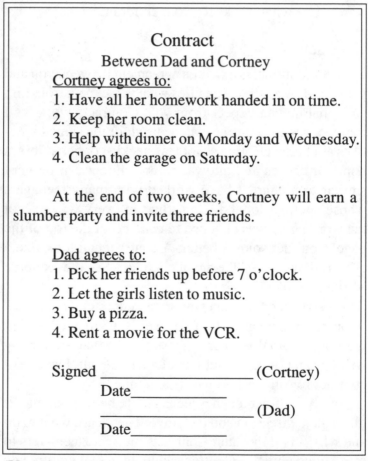

Contract
Between Dad and Cortney

Cortney agrees to:
1. Have all her homework handed in on time.
2. Keep her room clean.
3. Help with dinner on Monday and Wednesday.
4. Clean the garage on Saturday.

At the end of two weeks, Cortney will earn a slumber party and invite three friends.

Dad agrees to:
1. Pick her friends up before 7 o'clock.
2. Let the girls listen to music.
3. Buy a pizza.
4. Rent a movie for the VCR.

Signed _____ (Cortney)
       Date_____
       _____ (Dad)
       Date_____

(You may need to make a specific list for cleaning her room, helping with dinner and cleaning out the garage.)

Summary

Charts and contracts show your child's progress. Charts and contracts make your child feel successful. They emphasize achievements. Even if progress is slower than you would like, charts and contracts show where the gains occur. This gives you and your child incentive. It also helps you be patient. Here are some charts for you.

Top Ten Reasons to Use Charts and Contracts

Charts and contracts:

10. Solidify your improvement plan. They provide a picture of a behavioral agreement between you and your children.

9. Enable you to focus on specific, positive, priority behaviors and attitudes.

8. Provide a written record so you can evaluate progress.

7. Act as a tangible, visual reminder to be consistent. They give both parents the same tool.

6. Promote a positive family climate. Encourage everyone to work together.

5. Can be used to redirect inappropriate behavior. They can help improve poor days.

4. Encourage children to remember the rules. Teach children about accountability.

3. Create feelings of success and internal motivation which builds self-esteem.

2. Give children immediate, positive feedback on their accomplishments.

1. Give *PARENTS* immediate, positive feedback on their accomplishments.

Chart Making Guidelines

Create the chart with your child to insure interest and ownership.

Do not overload the chart with troublesome behaviors.

Maintain a high level of interest by changing priority behaviors occasionally.

Provide your child with a menu of incentives.

Weekend Menu

Overnight friend	15 points
Making popcorn	10 points
Ordering a pizza	30 points
Renting a movie	10 points
Playing miniature golf	25 points
Going out for lunch	30 points
Buying a new CD	30 points
Going to the zoo	15 points

Chapter 8

How To Use Rules And Consequences

Rules tell your children how you want them to behave. Rules are expectations. Expectations guide children's decision making. There are three factors to consider when developing expectations or rules. Expectations must be specific, reasonable and enforceable.

Expectations are *specific* when they communicate precisely what your child should or should not do. Most parents do not give their children clear and specific expectations. Clean your bedroom once a week. This is not specific. A specific expectation would be:

Bedroom cleaned every Saturday morning before noon.
Checklist:

> All dirty clothes put in the laundry basket.
> All furniture dusted and polished.
> Carpet vacuumed.
> Sheets changed.
> All toys in toybox.
> All clean clothes put away.

Look at expectations from your child's point of view. "Clean your room" can be vague and unclear. The task may look insurmountable to your child. A checklist gives your child exact steps to do — one at a time.

Expectations must be *reasonable*. Can your child accomplish the expectation or rule? The above checklist is specific, but it is unreasonable for a three-year-old. You can expect a young child to keep clothes and toys put away, but not dust and vacuum or change the sheets.

Expectations and rules must be *enforceable*. You can see when your child's bedroom is clean. The checklist is enforceable. Many parents have expectations that are not enforceable. This occurs often with teenagers. "You may never associate with Nicole again." This rule is not enforceable. You cannot follow your daughter around school. You cannot control all the places your daughter may associate with Nicole. It would be more enforceable to restrict Nicole from coming to your home. "You may not invite Nicole to our home."

A few, well-developed rules and expectations are better than many poorly developed ones. Have a set of rules. Have a rule for cooperation, listening the first time, or following directions. Have a rule for morning and evening routines. Have a rule about chores. Have a rule about homework time. Rules help you be consistent. They help you focus on priority behaviors.

Consequences Teach Decision-Making

Children earn positive consequences for choosing to follow rules. They earn negative consequences for not following rules. Consequences teach children how to make decisions. Good decisions result in positive consequences. Poor decisions result in negative consequences. Consequences teach children that there is cause-effect in the world. This is what happens when I choose this behavior.

Consequences must also be specific, reasonable and enforceable. A consequences is specific when the child knows exactly what is going to happen. If I choose this action, this will be the result. Consequences are reasonable when they make sense. Most parents are more reasonable when they are not angry.

Consequences must be enforceable. Choose consequences that you control. A physician asked my advice. He promised his twelve-year-old "anything he wanted" if he made the school honor roll. The boy made the honor roll and asked for a dune buggy. I told Dad he got off easy. The lad could have asked for a Porsche. Do not promise things you cannot deliver just to excite your child's motivation.

I was telling this story in class. A mother told her story from adolescence. Her father promised her a car if she improved in school. She explained how she remembered feeling. "Am I so bad and lazy that my father has to offer me a car to do better?" Her father's offer was well intended. It backfired. Promising a car was overdoing it. It was too much. It made her feel worse. It did not encourage her.

"It's Your Decision"

Use rules and consequences to teach your children that behaving in a responsible manner is their choice. Their choices determine their consequences. You do not.

"Stephanie, I would like you to be home for supper every day by 5 o'clock. I will trust you to be on time. You have shown a lot of responsibility lately. This will be an opportunity to prove your maturity." Mother gives Stephanie an incentive for being home on time. "If you are home on time, you can stay up an extra half hour and go out and play the next day." Mother explains the punishment. "If you choose to be late, you will go to bed at your regular time and not have playtime the next day. It's your decision." Stephanie agrees.

When Stephanie is home on time, Mother compliments her. If Stephanie comes home late, Mother could say, "I'm really sorry you were late, Stephanie. It's too bad you will miss the last half hour of your favorite show tonight. I really wanted you to see it."

Notice how this plan puts the responsibility on Stephanie, not Mom. Mom is still a nice person. She is on Stephanie's side. Stephanie makes the choice to go to bed early when she chooses to be late. Once expectations and consequences are set, stick to them. Be consistent. Be flexible before you establish expectations, not after an infraction.

Reality Consequences

You have read about tangible consequences and activity consequences in Chapter 6. Reality consequences occur naturally. A child who refuses to eat dinner goes hungry. A child who refuses to wash will develop body odor. When schoolmates begin commenting, the youngster will begin washing. Reality consequences also have positive results. A child who studies earns good grades. A child who does his chores earns an allowance. A youngster who exercises feels healthy. Reality consequences teach responsibility and decision-making because they permit children to learn from the real world. Use reality consequences whenever possible.

Summary

When expectations are too difficult, children become discouraged. Do not expect perfection. When expectations are too easy, children take advantage. Expectations are appropriate when children have to put forth effort without frustration.

Behavior is a choice. Tell your children how you expect them to behave. Then follow through with appropriate consequences. Be consistent with this technique and your children will make better decisions. They will choose responsible behavior.

Chapter 9

How To Be Proactive

To be proactive means to plan. Life is easier when you plan ahead. Many discipline problems can be avoided with a little planning. Planning makes use of the only advantage that we have over our children: experience. We are not more intelligent. They have more time and certainly more energy. If you plan, you will have fewer problems.

Anticipate

Suppose you are taking your children out for pizza. You know the restaurant will be crowded. There are many video games and other expensive distractions. You want your children to have fun, but you do not want to spend all your time chasing them around. Anticipate problems. Should I let them play games before the pizza is ready? How many games should I allow them to play? How long should we stay after we finish the pizza? Think ahead. Then tell your children exactly what you expect. Lay down the ground rules before you leave the house. Let them know what happens if they do not cooperate. Let them know what happens if they do cooperate.

> "You have had an excellent week, so we are going to Playtime Pizza for supper. You can play two video games while we are waiting for the pizza. If you listen to my directions, you can play two more games after we eat. I want you to have fun, but I also want you be behave. If you do a good job this time, I will want to take you

again some day. It's up to you. We'll be leaving in ten minutes."

Anticipate problems. You know the places where your children typically misbehave; the supermarket, church, and grandma's house. If you suspect there might be a problem, talk with your children before you leave. Tell them what you expect from them and what they can expect from you.

Think about your child's misbehavior. What are the recurring problems? What can you do to prevent these problems in the future? If your children argue, develop a plan to eliminate arguing. If your teenager is not motivated to do well in school, develop a plan that encourages motivation in school.

Proactive Shopping

Taking children shopping can be difficult. Children want everything they see. Stores are notorious for positioning items at child-eye level and within reach. Teach your children that they cannot always have everything they see. When Anthony was about four, I would take him on practice trips to the toy store. I would explain the rules before we left.

"How would you like to take a trip to the
    toy store?"
"Sure, Dad."
"We are going to look and play. But we are
    not going to buy anything."
"What do you mean?"
"We can go and have fun. But today is not
    for buying. Do you still want to go?"
"Yes."

We would go have fun at the toy store and leave without buying anything. Anthony would often ask to buy something just to see if I remembered. I would tell him not today. Maybe some other day. We would take these practice trips about once a month. Not only was I teaching him that you can not always buy what you want, we had a lot of fun in the process.

Planning for Improved Behavior

The following planning guide combines many of the ideas in this book into a set of specific strategies. This is a step-by-step method of planning. Follow these steps and behavior will improve.

Step 1: *Establish your goal.* How would you like things to be? What changes do you want to see in your children? When choosing a goal, base your decision on two factors. (1) Select a goal that offers a high chance of success. Your first plan must be successful. Success encourages more success. Do not start with the misbehavior that is most troublesome. (2) Select a goal that contributes to the success of the whole family. This will encourage a positive family climate.

Goal: Danny and Allison will get along with each other.

Step 2: *Make a list of specific behaviors that you want to increase or decrease.* What does getting along with each other really mean? What do you expect? These are your priority behaviors.
1. Danny and Allison will argue *less.*
2. Danny and Allison will tease each other *less.*
3. Danny and Allison will share each others' toys *more.*
4. Danny and Allison will call each other names *less.*
5. Danny and Allison will cooperate *more.*

Step 3: *Select one or two priority behaviors to change.* Choose behaviors that are easy to correct. Quick success is important.

<u>Step 4</u>: *Observe and keep a record for five days.* Once you have selected priority behaviors, count the number of times the behaviors occur each day. Do not do anything to change the behaviors. Simply observe them. You need to know how often the behaviors are occurring before you carry out the rest of the plan. This will enable you to evaluate your success.

Assume you have selected behaviors 1 and 3. Danny and Allison will argue less. Danny and Allison will share each others' toys more. Count and record the number of times Danny and Allison argue. Count and record the number of times they share toys. Do this for five days. Here is a record.

Behavior	Day 1	Day 2	Day 3	Day 4	Day 5
Argue	7	6	9	3	5
Share	1	0	2	0	0

Determine the current level of behavior before you begin applying consequences. This chart tells us that Danny and Allison argue an average of 6 times a day. They share less than once a day.

These records are very important. They will tell you if your plan is working. If you do not keep written records, you will be depending on your perception and memory. With some children, improvements come in small amounts. Some improvements are not easily detected. At the start of the plan, Danny and Allison are arguing an average of 6 times a day. Suppose that after two weeks, they are arguing 5 times a day. This is a small improvement. But it is still an improvement. If left to your perceptions, you would probably say the plan is not working.

You would be incorrect. You are making progress. The progress is so slight that you may not see it. Written records will show any amount of progress.

Step 5: *Decide how you will intervene*. What will you do to change the behaviors? What reinforcers will you use? What punishers will you use? Make a list of rewards and punishers. Ask your children for their ideas when you explain the plan. What incentives would they like to earn? Use charts, contracts and menus of incentives to give your plan power.

Step 6: *Explain the plan to your children*. Tell them your goal. Explain the priority behaviors. Establish the rules and consequences. Clarify what you expect from them and what they can expect from you. Be positive about the plan. Tell them that this is something that is going to make everyone feel better. Tell them you are serious about the plan. You will follow through with punishments if they choose to misbehave.

> "Children, I would like to talk to you about a new program. I expect that from now on, you will not argue. I also expect that you will share each others' toys. When you share and do not argue, you can earn extra minutes at story time. If you break a rule, you will go to time-out for five minutes. This plan will help you behave and get along with each other. I know you can do a good job."

From that moment, the choice to behave is with Danny and Allison. Mother can become a spectator, cheering for Danny and Allison to be winners, to be successful. When the children break a rule, Mother does not need to engage in lengthy arguments. Mother simply enforces the consequences. Mother is on their side. She is not the bad guy. Mother does not decide what happens. The children decide when they choose to behave or not.

Use plenty of encouragement. When your children show improvements, point out how well they are doing. Make comments that increase their self-worth. "It's good to see you sharing. You should both be proud of your behavior."

Step 7: *Evaluate*. Is this plan working? Observe and keep a record as you did in Step 4. By comparing these two sets of records, you will be able to determine if your plan is effective. Get your children involved in charting. Post the chart in the kitchen. Do a new chart each week.

When your children show improvements, add another priority behavior. Add another behavior but maintain the originals. If there is additional improvement next week, add another. Be cautious. It is better to add new behaviors slowly. Do not rush the plan. It may collapse. If there is no improvement after three weeks, adjust the plan.

Step 8: *Adjust the plan*. No improvement means the expectations are too high or the consequences are not motivating. If you think the expectations are too difficult, change them. If the children are unwilling to share each other's toys, you may change your expectation to taking turns while playing a game. Begin by playing the game with them. Model sharing and taking turns. Once they are successful, let them play a game alone. This expectation still emphasizes sharing and cooperation. As they learn to play more cooperatively, try sharing toys again.

The success of any plan depends on positive feedback and incentives. Children become tired of the same reward. Change incentives as needed to maintain a high level of motivation. See the list of incentives at the end of Chapter 6. If your children lose interest in story time, try a new incentive, such as happy faces or stickers on a chart. Old incentives lack power.

You may be tempted to use stronger punishments if your plan shows no improvement. Stronger punishments seldom help. Stronger punishments discourage most children. Children show less effort, not more effort. It is better to be consistent with one punishment and change the positive incentives.

When behaviors do not readily change, it is not because your child is terrible. It is not because you are a failure as a parent. When a behavior fails to change, it is because the system of expectations and consequences is not working properly.

Look at the plan. Should you make changes? Are you being consistent? Have you given the plan enough time? Are you protecting your button? Are consequences administered quickly? Are you giving negative attention? Are you ignoring? Are you catching your children being good? These questions will help you determine where your plan can be improved.

Summary

Successful parents plan ahead. They anticipate situations that may cause problems. If one or more of your children has a recurring misbehavior, develop a plan. Use the planning guide on the following pages to put your plan together.

Planning Guide

1. What behaviors do my children need to improve?

Goal: _____

2. List the specific behaviors you expect from your children.

_____

_____

_____

3. Choose one or two priority behaviors to change.

4. Keep a record. Count the number of times the priority behaviors occur each day.

Behavior	Day 1	Day 2	Day 3	Day 4	Day 5

5. What will I do?

Incentives _____
Charts _____
Contracts _____
Punishments _____

6. Explain the plan to your children. How can I get my children more involved in the plan? Outline what you want to say.

7. Evaluate. How will I know when the plan is working? Keep another record as you did in step 4. Count the number of times the priority behaviors occur each day.

Behavior	Day 1	Day 2	Day 3	Day 4	Day 5

8. How will I adjust the plan? What other consequences can I use? Ask yourself these questions:

Am I being consistent with positive feedback?
Have I given the plan enough time to work?
Am I following through with punishment?
Am I getting angry?
Am I yelling?

Chapter 10

How To Motivate Your Children

"My son won't do anything."

"What do you mean?"

"All he does is watch TV."

"Does he have any responsibilities around the house?"

"Yes. But getting him to do them is a struggle. Everything is a struggle."

"How does he do in school?"

"He passes. He could do better if he worked a little. He is so unmotivated."

All children are motivated. Not all children are motivated to behave and work hard. Some children are motivated to do nothing. Think about motivation in two ways. Some motivation comes from inside you — it is internal. Some motivation comes from outside you — it is external. Being overweight is bad for your heart. Losing weight to improve your health requires internal motivation. You have a desire to lose weight. Losing weight to win a bet is an example of external motivation.

Most of us get up and go to work each day for two reasons. We get personal satisfaction from our work — internal. We also get paid — external. We need both. Most of us do not drive at 100 miles per hour. We know it is unsafe — internal. We do not want to go to jail — external. Internal and external motivation work together to produce a responsible person.

Emphasize Success

Success creates internal motivation. When your boss praises your work, you feel successful and continue to work hard. You can use success to give your child a boost of internal motivation. Point out your child's good behavior and decisions. Your child will feel successful. Success motivates him to work harder. When you compliment your child for having a clean bedroom, he will feel good inside — he will feel successful. He will be more motivated to keep his room clean.

Many children believe they cannot be successful. This false belief usually comes from repeated failures. Sometimes it is the result of high expectations. Correct this problem by spotlighting the positive. Point out strengths. Show your child where he has made progress. Encourage him to believe in himself. This will help your child feel success. Once success gets started, it continues. Success breeds success.

Develop expectations that build on success. This strategy is called *shaping*. When you are teaching a complex behavior, divide the task into small sequential steps. Expect progress not perfection. Consider this example.

Liz would like to teach Carlos how to get ready for school. This includes getting washed, brushing his teeth, getting dressed and making his bed. Liz decides that getting washed by himself has first priority. It may take a few days or a few weeks before Carlos becomes proficient at washing. Once accomplished, Liz teaches Carlos to brush his teeth and get dressed. Finally, Liz teaches Carlos to make his bed.

The small sequence of steps improves the probability of success. Placing all the tasks on Carlos would have been unreasonable. It may have resulted in frustration and failure. Shaping takes time. It is a good method of teaching.

Use shaping to improve behavior gradually. Shaping means encouraging better effort. Suppose your child takes 40 minutes to do a chore that should take 10 minutes. Set a timer and play "Beat the Clock." Reinforce him for completing the job within the limit. Starting with a time limit of 10 minutes may cause failure. To improve the chances for success, start with a time limit of 30 minutes. This is still an improvement over 40 minutes. After a week, move the limit to 25 or 20 minutes. Gradually, you will achieve the 10 minute goal. Shaping improves the chance of successful behavior.

When teaching new expectations, reinforce improvements or steps in the right direction. Do not insist on perfect performance on first attempts. Just because you have taught your five-year-old how to make his bed, do not expect him to do the job as well as you. He will be happy with a lumpy bedspread. He will steadily improve with your guidance and encouragement.

A child who misbehaves frequently lacks the internal motivation to cooperate. Use praise and encouragement to get success started. Once he experiences good behavior, he will be more motivated to behave in the future. Tell your child when he is doing well. That will motivate him further.

Parents have a tendency to focus on negative behavior. We tell our children what they are doing wrong. Misbehaviors get our attention. Many parents believe that being critical of mistakes is one way to instill more effort. This is not true. Focus on what your children do well.

Your son does a mediocre job sweeping the garage. "You didn't sweep the corners at all. You're so lazy. A six-year-old could do better." This type of criticism is not motivating. This is better. "You got the middle part okay. You missed some dirt in the corners. I'll do one corner to show you how. Then you can do the rest. Do the corners as well as you did the middle and it will look great." This comment is encouraging. It builds success. Success motivates children to work harder.

At times, you may need incentives that are stronger than praise and encouragement. Incentives can be an allowance, toys, or privileges. Use charts and contracts. Make an agreement with your child. Have a good week in school and we will do something special on Saturday. Children like working toward a goal. Do not set the standards too high. This can create too much pressure and have a reverse effect on motivation. Do not expect perfect behavior for two months before you allow your daughter to go to the movies. You are expecting too much.

Whenever you use incentives such as rewards or privileges, always accompany the incentive with verbal encouragement. Always remind your child that the reason to behave and work hard is to feel good about yourself. Aim for self reward. That is always more important than the actual incentive.

> "I hope you feel good about your week in school. You should be proud of yourself. A little hard work really pays off. I'm glad you earned the movie on Saturday. But, I hope you understand that the best reason to do well in school is you. Do well in school because it is good for you. You are more important than the movie."

Use Interest

Interest creates motivation. Suppose that you are trying to improve your child's reading skills. You know that your child likes dinosaurs. By reading books about dinosaurs, you will increase your child's motivation. Your child's interest in dinosaurs makes the reading meaningful and fun. Your child is motivated to learn because he is interested in what he is reading. (There is a questionnaire at the end of this chapter that will help you discover and stay in touch with your child's interests.)

Make learning interesting. With young children, you can make changes in a child's behavior by playing a game. Pat taught Katie how to make her bed by playing role reversal. Katie played the mom and mom played the child. Katie liked being the mother, so making the bed became a fun-filled activity.

Family Climate

A pleasant family climate motivates children. Family climate refers to the way everyone in the family feels about each other. Pleasant family climate develops in families where members speak politely to each other and discipline is positive. Everyone feels a sense of togetherness and cooperation. Structure is balanced with flexibility. Everyone is encouraged to pursue their own interests. The family has fun together; they have inside jokes. When the climate is warm and accepting, children learn your values and goals. Children are willing to accept guidance and punishment because they see that you are acting out of love and concern. If a problem occurs, the children will rebound more quickly.

Unpleasant family climate develops in families where there is anger and criticism. The rules and structure are rigid — there is no room for individual flexibility. Everyone becomes defensive. The parents see more bad than good. The children are always picking on each other.

Family climate begins with parents who are good models. Teach your children to thank people who are nice to them. Teach them to apologize to those they hurt. Teach them to be empathic. Teach them to comfort others who are not doing well. The best way to teach these qualities is by living them yourself. Do not complain about helping Grandma with her shopping. Explain that helping others makes you feel good inside — that's the reward.

Make your children feel secure and safe. Children like everything in the family to run smoothly. Children worry about changes. Children worry about changes at school. They worry when Dad gets a new job. Explain changes before they happen. Reassure your children that you will always love them.

Look for family climate the next time you go shopping. Find a place to sit and watch families. When you see a family walking together and talking nicely to one another, you are looking at pleasant family climate. If you hear the parents say, "Stand up straight when you walk. Hold on to that package, I don't want to lose it. Walk over here with us," you are looking at unpleasant family climate. If you hear the children say, "I'm telling. You're in trouble. Tell her to stop teasing me. Look what he is doing, Mom," you are looking at unpleasant family climate.

Pleasant climate can be disrupted by a negative situation, such as an argument between two children. If a situation creates an unpleasant family climate, put it behind you. Change the subject. Think of something positive. Return to a pleasant family climate as soon as possible. If two of your children have an argument, help them reach a settlement. Then redirect their energy. You may need to stay with them for a while to insure better feelings toward each other. Go for a walk. Read a story. Get them involved in something pleasant.

Family climate can fluctuate. Some days climate is pleasant, other days it is not. This is normal. Aim for more good days than bad days. If one parent promotes a pleasant climate and the other does not, the children will adjust. Make your time with the children pleasant. Some pleasant climate is better than none.

The Benefit of Humor

One important aspect of pleasant family climate is humor. Humor can redirect family climate. When everyone is feeling down, a little humor helps turn things around. Humor can also redirect misbehavior. This works especially well with young children. "Is that your Grinch face? What happened? What turned your smile face into a Grinch face?" If your child is familiar with the story of Snow White, you can make comparisons with Grumpy and Happy.

You can also use humor for occasional forgetfulness. Your child forgets to sweep the patio. Leave him a note. "I hope you have a nice day on the PATIO!" You may want to tape the note to the broom handle and set it by his bedroom door. This only works well if your child has honestly forgotten. If he "forgot" because he did not feel like sweeping the patio, humor is not appropriate. Punishment is appropriate.

Not all mischief is misbehavior. Children can get into plenty of trouble without intending misbehavior. Mary had four young children. One day, the middle two wanted to be mommy's helper. Mom was busy with an ill baby. So they decided to wash the kitchen tile. They had seen mom wash the tile before. They were sure they knew what to do. One went for the mop and pail while the other went for the vinegar. They had seen mom use vinegar to clean the floors. Mary heard the commotion in the kitchen. She put the baby down. She hurried to see what was happening. When her first foot hit the kitchen floor, it slid out from under her. She slid half way across the floor. Next to the vinegar, Mary kept the olive oil. At least she used to.

Summary

Point out things your children do well. This makes them feel successful. Success encourages children to be more motivated. Interesting activities encourage children to enjoy learning. Maintaining a pleasant family climate helps children develop cooperation. These factors increase motivation, improve decision making and promote good behavior.

YOUR TURN

Make a list of activities you can do to create and maintain a pleasant family climate. Here are some ideas to get you started:

Play games
Read stories
Tell jokes
Go for a walk and talk
Discussions at the dinner table
Be helpful to each other
Listen to music
Practice giving compliments to each other

Write your ideas here:

Test Your Knowledge about Your Child's Interests

Knowing your child's interests helps you create motivating activities. Make two or more copies of this page. Think about one of your children. Answer each question below as though your child were answering the question. When you are finished, ask your child to answer each question. When he has finished, compare your answers to his. If your child is too young, read the questions to him, but no coaching.

1. My favorite TV show is
2. What I like best about myself is
3. My favorite thing to eat for supper is
4. My favorite color is
5. Other kids think I am
6. My favorite song is
7. What I like best about my mother is
8. My best school subject is
9. My favorite video game is
10. When I have to work around the house, I
11. What I like best about my father is
12. I like my teacher when
13. My favorite movie is
14. I think my bedtime should be
15. When I have free time, I like to
16. When I grow up, I want to
17. I like people who
18. What I would like to change about me is
19. I do not like people who
20. If I had lots of money, I would

This exercise is not as easy as it first appears. Do not be surprised if you match only five or six answers. More than eight is great. If you want to know what motivates your children, you need to know their interests. This activity can help you understand more about your children. Repeat the activity with each of your children. You may also repeat the activity every few months. Make up your own questions. Many parents have told me that their children made a questionnaire for them. Have fun.

Family Climate Comparisons

For several years, I would ask parents who were taking my workshop to write down two or three words to describe a pleasant family climate and an unpleasant family climate. Here are the results. Remember that your goal is to keep your family's climate on the plus side as much as possible. When you have a bad climate day, put it behind you. Humor often helps.

Pleasant Family Climate	Unpleasant Family Climate
Warmth	Separate
Loving	Aloofness
Closeness	Distance
Consistent	Unpredictable
Supportive	Fear
Understanding	Hurt
Encouraging	Criticism
Open communication	Closed communication
Okay to feel	Deny feelings
Accepting	Rejection
Concerned	Selfish
Respectful	Hostility
Cooperation	Control
Quality time	Tension
Humor	Anger
Fun	Chaos
Happiness	Sadness
High self-esteem	Withdrawal
Strength	Poor coping

Chapter 11

Self Esteem - Motivation's Heartbeat

Here is a teenager with poor self-esteem describing himself.

> "I don't like myself much. I'm not a very popular kid. I'm not very good at sports. Who cares? My grades are average. There are a lot of things I don't want to do. I just don't understand them. I don't like trying new things; they scare me. I hate making decisions. What if I make the wrong choice? I'm not real confident."

Here is a teenager with healthy self-esteem.

> "I'm a pretty good kid I guess. I have a few good friends. Sometimes they listen to me. I like sports but I'm not that great. I wish I had more time to do all the stuff I want to do. There are so many new things to learn about. Making decisions does not scare me. If I mess up, no problem. I'll figure something out to make it work."

What is Self-Esteem?

Simply stated, your self-esteem is your attitude or belief about yourself. People with healthy self-esteem respect themselves. They control their behavior. They are confident about their decisions. Children who believe in themselves expect success from life. They feel good about themselves. They are confident. They can take constructive criticism. I have never worked with a child who was feeling good about himself and misbehaving at the same time.

People with poor self-esteem have little self-respect. They are unsure of their actions and decisions. Children with poor self-esteem have difficulty learning. They feel insecure. They lack persistence. They are over-sensitive to what others think. They blame others when things go wrong.

Children with poor self-esteem see the world as a place to fear. They feel unworthy. They have low self-confidence and do not have faith in themselves. Since these children see themselves as failures, they expect failure and behave accordingly. When this happens, these children simply stop trying. They stop putting forth effort. For children who feel insecure, the surest way to avoid failure and embarrassment is to avoid participation. Nothing ventured, nothing failed. Not trying makes more sense than trying hard and then failing anyway. Then the child can say, "Well I didn't even try." This is better than saying, "I tried hard but failed."

Your goal as a person should be to strive for healthier self-esteem. Your goal as a parent is to promote healthy self-esteem in your children. Give your child support and encouragement and your child will develop healthy self-esteem.

A child falls while learning to ride a bike. "That's not how to do it. I've explained this once already. Pay attention this time." These comments reduce self-esteem. Here is a more productive comment. "Good try. You are doing better each time. I know you can do it." This reaction shows confidence in your child's abilities. It persuades your child to believe in himself.

There is extensive evidence connecting poor self-esteem with drug and alcohol abuse. Teenagers place high value on what other teenagers think about them. This is natural. Adolescents with good self-esteem have a stronger sense of self-worth. They can resist peer pressure. Since they like themselves, they are less fearful of not being liked by others.

Teenagers with poor self-esteem need peer approval. Since they do not like themselves very much, they need others to like them. The easiest way to get approval is to go along with the crowd. Having friends in a gang or friends who use drugs feels better than not having friends.

How to Develop Healthy Self-Esteem in Your Children

Show your child that he is an important person by treating him with respect. The "spilled milk" example illustrates this point. Suppose you invited your pastor to dinner. During dinner, he spills a glass of milk. How would you react? "Accidents will happen. Don't worry, it happens all the time. Here, I'll get it. Let me clean it up." How do you react when your child spills a glass of milk. "Not again! I told you to be more careful. You are so clumsy. You've ruined the tablecloth."

Accept and love your children just the way they are. This does not mean that you have to love their misbehavior. Love your child regardless of his misbehavior. "I love you. I do not like what you did." This message lets your child know that you love him, but you do not like the misbehavior.

Teach your children that effort is essential to success. Persistence pays off. "Getting a good grade on the science test will not be easy. You will have to study hard. You're clever enough to know that the hard work will be worth it. I am sure you will do just fine." Encourage your children and they will see that you have faith and confidence in them. Encouragement will help your children face situations with more confidence.

Do not do things for your children that they can do for themselves. Being overprotective can cause children to feel insecure or lazy. They will learn to depend on you to do things for them.

Teach your children to accept their weaknesses along with their strengths. Children with poor self-esteem only pay attention to their weaknesses. Since they dwell on their shortcomings, their positive qualities are overlooked. Explain that everyone has strong qualities and weak qualities. Use yourself as an example.

Anthony was disappointed in himself for not playing better basketball. I explained that each person has things they do well and things they do not do well. I used myself as an example. When I was his age, I was often disappointed. I wanted to be stronger, more coordinated and more athletic. Sharing my experience teaches him that it is normal to feel disappointed — but be careful. Do not say, "I was never good in math. You won't be either." This will set your child up for failure.

Teach your children to overcome disappointments. Disappointments are part of life. We all have them. Teach children to experience their disappointments without the results being tragic.

Todd was seventeen. He lived day to day without much purpose until he met Michelle. They fell in love. Todd was awe struck. Someone loved him. He invested his whole life in Michelle. He loved her to the exclusion of all else. She was his sole reason to live. He spent every minute thinking of her. Then she dumped him. No Michelle. No reason to live. His life became meaningless. He could not put the pieces of his life together. There were too many pieces missing. Todd escaped into drugs for two years. He suffered. He was alone. One day he realized he was killing himself. He got help. He survived.

Whenever you trust your feelings of self worth to someone else, you risk being hurt. Self esteem roots must grow deep within yourself. It's wonderful to feel loved. That cannot be denied. Teach your children that it is important to love and support yourself; to be your own best friend.

Teach children to appreciate reasons for life. Reasons for relationships. Reasons to go to school. Reasons to work. Teach them alternatives. If one reason fails, tragedy will not result.

Scott was a junior in high school. He lived to play football. He was a good player. College material. Maybe pro. He was very popular. He hung out with the jocks and cheerleaders. He was invited to all the important parties. Then he was injured. No football for the rest of his life. No practices. No football buddies. No cheers. No glory after the victories. No reason to go to school. No reason to live.

Scott had all his self-esteem in one basket. When that was taken away, he had no other way to feel good about himself. There was no purpose without football. He had no alternatives. He tried to kill himself but failed. Scott got lucky. Then he got help. It took Scott a year of therapy to see any value in his life.

Summary

You must take an active role in building your children's self-esteem. Provide encouragement and support. Give your children positive feedback whenever possible. Tell your children that they have the power to behave. Teach them to have self-confidence. Believe in your children and they will learn to believe in themselves. That's the best motivation there is.

Chapter 12

Being Consistent Can Make You Feel Dreadful

One evening, the four of us went out for dinner. Leah was three years old. The children knew that after dinner, we often have dessert. Leah ordered her usual cheeseburger and fries and small milk with one straw. For whatever reason, Leah wanted to look around the restaurant more than eat. We gave her the familiar reminders. With each reminder, she took another nibble of her burger or sip of her milk. She was not eating very well. Meanwhile, the rest of us were nearly finished.

Realizing that she was not hungry, I wanted to be reasonable. I cut the remainder of her burger in half. "You have to eat this half of your burger before it's time for dessert. If you do not eat, you will not get ice cream." Leah smiled and agreed but continued to look around and not eat. Soon, the time of reckoning was upon us. It was time to order dessert.

We thought about buying her some ice cream anyway. Although she had not eaten, she was polite and well behaved. We thought about the scene she would create when she found out she does not get any ice cream. We thought about how embarrassed we would be. Many parents think this way. This is how we justify giving in, especially in public. Do not give in to these thoughts.

Our only alternative was to follow through. If you do not eat — no dessert. Consistency is more important than a few tears and some embarrassment. Our choice was not what to do, but how to do it. We decided that Mom and Anthony would get three ice-cream cones and meet me at the checkout counter. I would remain at the table and give Leah more time to eat. Not because she could still get ice cream. It was too late for that. I wanted her to eat more of her dinner. The deadline for getting ice cream had expired.

After a few more minutes, I told Leah we were leaving. She asked if she could have her ice cream now. I said "No, you did not finish your dinner." "I'll eat it now, Daddy," she pleaded. Then she saw three ice-cream cones, not four. We softly explained that we finished our dinners. That's why we each had ice cream.

As I carried my screaming daughter under my arm past a crowded dining room of families, I felt dreadful. I wondered what they were thinking. I wanted to explain. "It's okay, I'm just being consistent."

Leah cried and pleaded all the way home. She said she would eat her dinner if we would only give her another chance. All this sadness while three of us were choking on our ice cream. Anthony wanted to give her some of his. It was the first time in my life I did not enjoy eating ice cream. I wanted to roll down my window and toss it out. We love Leah. Watching her cry was excruciating.

Think About the Future

Sometimes, saying no and being consistent is not easy. It can hurt. It would have been much easier to give in and buy the ice cream. We did not. We knew it was more important to be consistent. Even though being consistent is sometimes painful.

We wanted Leah to learn that Mom and Dad mean what they say. Even if it means some temporary unpleasantness. You have to eat your dinner if you want dessert. If you do not finish your dinner, you will not keep the rest of us from having dessert. You have to do what you are asked, even in a public place.

About two weeks later, we returned to the same restaurant. We wanted to see if our struggle had any effect. Leah ate with purpose. Occasionally, she would pause and say, "I'm gonna eat all my cheeseburger tonight." When the waitress delivered her ice cream, it was a double treat. Leah was happy and proud of herself. We knew that our painful experience had paid off.

Do not let little misbehaviors slide. They grow into larger problems. When we followed through with Leah, we were thinking about the future more than the present. We wanted Leah to know that she had to eat her dinner this time and every time.

What Happens When You Do Not Follow Through

Anna's ten-year-old son, Joel, played outside each day after school. When Joel came inside for dinner, he was supposed to wash his hands before coming to the table. Every day, Joel came to the table without washing his hands. Anna would say, "Please go wash your hands." Joel would go wash his hands. He never argued about it. He was always cooperative once Anna reminded him. This went on for weeks. Joel came to the table with dirty hands. Anna would send him to wash. One day, Anna confronted Joel. "Every day, you come to the table without washing your hands, and every day, I send you to the bathroom. Can you explain why you don't wash your hands first?" Joel immediately looked up at his mom. "One day you didn't catch me."

"One day you didn't catch me." It may have been six weeks ago, but he got away with it one time. One time he was able to eat dinner without washing — without being caught. What a thrill! This story shows how children think.

It shows how their clever minds work. It made more sense to come to the table and be sent away than wash his hands the first time around. Why? Because he got away with it one time. One slip and Joel tests Anna for weeks, just to see if she will slip again. That is why consistency is so important.

This story reminds me of Las Vegas. People put coin after coin into the slot machines. The occasional pay-off is worth the gamble. Coming to the table with dirty hands was a gamble. It was a gamble worth taking.

Most parents are not consistent. We say things we don't mean. We say "no" and then give in. We don't follow through. With a little teasing, most of us change "no" to "yes". Some days we let misbehaviors slide. Some days we play warden.

The Difference Between Threats and Warnings

Threats are not punishments. A threat is an intention to punish. Big difference. Threats are just words. Many parents threaten because they do not know how to use punishment. Some parents threaten because they are afraid to use punishment. Some parents threaten because the are too lazy to follow through with a punishment. Whatever the reason, threats often make a child's misbehavior worse.

Have you ever been in a waiting room where there were parents and young children? "If you do not sit down I will put you in the car." The child sits for a minute or two and then starts jumping around again. Mom threatens. The child sits a few minutes and then gets up. Mom threatens again, etc.

Threats teach your children not to believe what you say. Children know that threats are not always enforced. How do they know? You have not persisted in the past. You have not followed through. Threatening is a magnified form of inconsistency.

Warnings are a little different. Warnings can be effective if you use them sparingly and with plenty of judgment. Most children do not need warnings. Most children know what is proper behavior and what is not. Use a warning only when your child does not know that he is behaving inappropriately. "Ben! That is not acceptable. Please stop."

Not all parents can use warnings successfully. Only parents who have a reputation for following through can use warnings. Parents often ask what the difference is between a threat and a warning. The distinction is not found in what the parent says. The distinction is found in what your child hears.

Melody brought four-year-old David to our house for a birthday party. Midway through the party, David began to act up. Melody warned him to stop. He did not. Melody told him that they would leave the party. He continued to misbehave. She picked him up and headed for the car. He cried and pleaded to stay. They left and did not return. The party was over for David. Even though Melody also had to leave, she followed through. David has been good at parties ever since.

If you have consistently followed through with what you say, your child will hear a warning. Your child has learned that when you say "stop" you mean stop now. If you have been inconsistent, your child will only hear a threat when you say "stop." Your child has learned that it takes several threats before he actually has to stop.

There is another type of warning that can be used effectively. This is a time warning. Time warnings are very helpful for parents and children. Here are some examples.

"Dinner will be ready in 10 minutes. Please finish your game and wash-up by then."

"You can play until the timer goes off. I'll set it for 15 minutes."

"Mom's taxi leaves in 7 minutes. All aboard by then!"

Time warnings let your children know ahead of time that something is expected of them very soon. This is less of a surprise and generally encourages them to be more cooperative. I am not sure why, but for some reason, children love timers. You can use the timer on the oven, a bell timer or an egg timer. The feedback I have received from parents confirms my belief in time warnings and timers. Most parents have found these techniques to be very helpful.

"Five More Minutes," "Maybe," and "We'll See"

Many parents are afraid to say no. Some parents do not say no because they want to avoid an argument. Some parents feel embarrassed or guilty if their child has a tantrum. Some parents are afraid of being disliked by their children. Some parents are lazy and do not want to take firm action. So parents use stall statements. Most of us learn stall statements from our parents. "Five more minutes," "Maybe" and "We'll see" are three favorite stall statements. They are among the most commonly used words in America.

"It's time to go home."
"Can't we stay a little while longer?"
"Okay, five more minutes."

"Can we have some ice cream after supper?"
"Maybe."

"Can we go to the park tomorrow, Dad?"
"We'll see."

Stall statements delay the inevitable. It is okay to use delays as long as your children know that "maybe" sometimes means yes and sometimes means no. Your children must realize that "we'll see" sometimes means yes and sometimes means no. Your children must understand that "five more minutes" means five more minutes, not ten more minutes.

Using stall statements occasionally is harmless. Use them too often and your children will whine and plead and beg, hoping you will give in. Use them carefully.

How do you teach your children that maybe sometimes means no. Every now and then, follow a maybe with a no. "I know I said maybe. I have thought about it. The answer is no." You may find that your children will not like hearing this. That's all right. They will live. Be consistent. It will be worth it in the long run.

What Consistency Means to Your Children

If you want self-disciplined children, you need to be consistent. You need to mean what you say. You need to follow through. You can significantly improve your children's behavior by being more positive and more consistent. All parents need to be more consistent. Consistency is the most important element in your relationship with your children. It is the most important ingredient, yet it is the most frequently omitted. If you change one thing about the way you discipline your children, be more consistent.

Corrine was not a strong disciplinarian. Her fourteen-year-old daughter, Joanne, behaved anyway she pleased. Joanne would stay up past midnight, watching TV and talking on the telephone. She was always late for school. She refused to do housework. She argued about everything. Joanne ruled the home. Joanne always got her way. Corrine always gave in. Corrine and I had several meetings. We talked about consistency and follow through. We developed a plan that gave Corrine authority. Corrine learned to follow-through with mild restrictions whenever Joanne misbehaved. Gradually, Corrine saw some improvements. I asked Corrine to bring Joanne to our next session. I asked Joanne how things were going at home. She responded with a glare, "Horrible since my mother started talking to you." I couldn't help but smile.

Consistency means follow through. Manage a misbehavior exactly the same way every time it occurs. This is especially true when working with persistent misbehaviors. Once you tell your daughter to be home at 5 o'clock, follow through if she is late. Some parents justify being a little late to avoid a conflict. "It's not that big a problem." "I'm too tired to deal with this now." You are fooling yourself. How big must the problem be in order for you to act? Will you be less tired tomorrow?

You set the speed limit. Freeway drivers know that the true speed limit is 74 not 65. Most police do not give tickets until you are traveling 74. If you can drive 74 without penalty, you will. This is the same for children. If you set the speed limit at 65, follow through at 66. If you give a little leeway, they will push for more.

When you are consistent with one child, other children learn by observing. During my first summer working at a home for boys, I was taking a van full of children on a weekend camp out. After a few miles of travel, Lamont started getting restless. I gave him a warning. About 50 miles from home, he began teasing and instigating. I gave him another warning. He was getting worse. I told him that if he did not stop, I would turn the van around and take him back home. He did not believe me. He did not think I would follow through. He did not stop. I did. I turned the van around. What a shock. First, he stopped misbehaving. Then he started pleading with me that he would be good. "Too late," I said. Home he went.

It took about two hours to take Lamont home and then return to the place where I had turned around. Those were two of the best hours I ever spent. My reputation with Lamont and all the other children was made that day. Not only did the rest of the trip go smoothly, but for the next six years, the story was handed down from child to child. "You better believe what Mr. Sal tells you. He means it."

I have often wondered what would have happened if I had not turned around. Lamont would have continued to misbehave. The other children would have seen that I give threats but do not follow through. They would have started testing me. The weekend would have been a disaster for all of us, particularly me.

When a misbehavior occurs, deal with it now. If you let it slide, you will pay the price in the future. Do not let friends, neighbors or grandparents influence your commitment to be consistent. "Let it go this time." "How often do we get to see him." "He's okay. He's just a little excited." You are the parent. You do what is best for your children. Let other people raise their children. You be consistent. Children love to get away with misbehaviors. It is your job to see that they do not.

Children learn to make decisions by predicting the consequences of their actions. Children learn self-discipline by predicting the outcome of their behavior. They must be able to see the cause-effect relationship between how they behave and what happens to them. If I choose this behavior, then this consequence will happen.

Your children must be able to predict your reaction to their behavior. They need to know how you behave. They need to know the consequences. Children will learn this cause-effect relationship more quickly when you behave consistently.

Consistency Between Parents

Becky was two. Her mother and father were sitting on the couch. Becky asked Mom for some yogurt. Mom said "No, it is too close to dinner." Without a moment's hesitation, Becky turned to Dad and asked him for some yogurt. If one parent says no, try the other. Children learn to manipulate at a young age. It gets worse as they grow older. "I knew I should have asked Dad first."

Consistency is important between parent and child. It is also important between parent and parent. If Dad is too easy and Mom is too strict, your children will quickly learn to manipulate. If your speed limit is 40 and dad's is 65, your children will learn to take advantage. This is disastrous. Children will learn which parent to ask for what things. When you want a treat, more TV time, or a couple of extra dollars, ask Dad. He usually gives in on these matters. When you want to postpone doing a chore or have a friend spend the night, ask Mom. She's easy.

Agree on the house rules and expectations. Agree on what children earn and do not earn. Agree on how and when to use punishment. Agree on things that relate to discipline. If you disagree, that's fine. Disagree behind closed doors. Work things out when your children are not around. Even if you do not agree, present a united front to your children. Compromise if you must. If you disagree in front of your children, you will be teaching them where you are vulnerable. Then you will hear statements such as, "Well, Dad thinks it's okay," or "Mom said I could go."

100

Talk with your spouse about discipline. Explore each other's feelings and beliefs. Review your ideas periodically. Make a list of misbehaviors. Have a strategy that deals with each misbehavior. That way, whichever parent is around, misbehavior will be handled consistently. When unplanned situations occur, wait for your spouse. Simply say, "I'll have to talk with your father before making a decision. You will have to wait." Children learn that you mean business with this approach. They will learn that you are working together. They will not be tempted to play one of you against the other.

Do not confuse this suggestion with "Wait until your father gets home." Do not depend on one parent to make all the decisions about discipline. Only special problems need to be discussed. Day-to-day discipline must be handled immediately. If Mom depends on Dad to be the heavy, the children will seldom listen to Mom. Mom must take charge of her time with the children.

Summary

Consistency is not always easy, but it is always worth it. Think of the future. Do not let little problems grow. Deal with misbehavior immediately. Do not be afraid to say no. Talk with your spouse about discipline, even if you are divorced. Plan to manage misbehaviors consistently.

Chapter 13

How To Be More Consistent

Mrs. Ellis and her five children moved into a school where I worked. Within the first week, each child had been sent to the principal at least once. I asked Mrs. Ellis to meet with me. She agreed. I began to give her my pep talk on consistency. She interrupted. "I know I need to be consistent," she said. "Right now I am tired. I need a little vacation from consistency."

She had five children who needed consistent follow through. It took a lot out of her to be consistent. Every now and then, she let go. She gave up. Not completely. Just temporarily. That was the problem.

You cannot be consistent some of the time. You must be consistent all the time. That is not easy. It is exhausting. It drains your energy. It weakens your spirit. Here are seven strategies that will help you be more consistent.

Emphasize Priority Behaviors

The first strategy that will help you be more consistent is the idea of priority behavior. A priority behavior is a behavior that you are going to manage with special diligence and focus. A priority behavior can be positive. If you want your children to cooperate with each other, cooperation is the priority behavior. So you focus on cooperation. Catch your children cooperating. This will teach your children that you value cooperation.

A priority behavior can be a misbehavior. Many children develop misbehavior patterns. They display the same misbehavior repeatedly. Examples are arguing, whining and disobeying. Your child may exhibit several misbehavior patterns. Attempting to work on all misbehaviors at once would be impossible for you and confusing for your child. Choose one or two patterns as priority misbehaviors. Be aware of these misbehaviors at all times. Never give in. Do not reward them. Be consistent. This will not be easy. There will be times when you are tired and will not want to follow through. If you do not, you will pay for it later.

Priority behaviors help you focus. It is difficult to be consistent with every misbehavior. Identify one or two priority behaviors and focus your energy on them. Be consistent and diligent with priority behaviors. Your children will learn to behave more quickly.

Remember to be positive. Every misbehavior has an opposite, positive behavior. Watch for positive behaviors while you are consistent with priority misbehaviors. Suppose your child's priority misbehavior is having tantrums. Be consistent and never reward the priority misbehavior. Never reward any tantrum. You must also reinforce your child for not having tantrums. "I'm glad to see that you did not cry when I told you that you could not have a candy bar. I really appreciate that. Thank you."

When you are consistent with priority behaviors, it will have a positive effect on all other behaviors. Your children will generalize what they learn from one situation to another. It is like having a two-for-one sale on good behavior. Be consistent with priority behaviors and get improvement in other behaviors free. How could you refuse such a deal?

Give Yourself Tangible Reminders.

Using tangible reminders is the second strategy that helps you be more consistent. Write little notes to yourself. "Do not give in to tantrums." "Catch your children playing quietly." Put a sign on your bathroom mirror. "Look for cooperation." Put a sign on the refrigerator. "Stay calm. Do not argue." Notes and signs help you remember to be consistent. They help you remember to focus on priority behaviors.

I learned this my first year teaching. Kenny and Aaron were my two top students. They were thirteen. Handsome. Articulate. Leaders. They were very much alike. That was their problem. They hated each other. They were on each other's case constantly. I tried being positive. I was not consistent enough. It was too hard. I had tunnel vision. I could only see the misbehavior. I had to do something. I decided to put a sign in the back of my classroom.

> Catch Kenny and Aaron
> being pleasant to each other!!

It was like magic. The sign was not to remind Kenny and Aaron to be pleasant to each other. The sign was to help me be consistent and positive. It helped me focus on a positive behavior. The class thought it was a dumb idea at first. By the end of the week, every student in my class wanted their own sign on the wall. They loved all the attention. I loved all the cooperation and good behavior.

Practice Patience

The third strategy that you need to be more consistent is patience. Parents want quick changes — children do not. Children do not change misbehavior patterns easily. Misbehaviors that have been mastered take time to give up. Just because you decide to be consistent, your child's misbehavior will not change overnight. You will have to be patient.

Patience is difficult. You want immediate results for your energy and commitment. Think about things from your child's point of view. If you have been using threats and warnings before taking action, your child has learned that this is how you behave. Now, you have changed. You are consistent. You are following through. Your child will be confused and resist change. "I don't understand this, Dad. You always yell three or four times before you really mean it." It takes time and energy to change your behavior. Your child is no different. Be patient.

Choose a Good Time

If you are going to initiate a new plan or start a new discipline technique with your children, choose a good time to begin. An experienced mom gave me this idea. She was taking my parenting class during the early Spring. She was a tax accountant. She explained that she had learned never to start anything new during tax season. She was working 60 plus hours per week. She was not at her best at home. She recognized that this period was not a good time to make any new resolutions, start a diet, change a bad habit, or try to enforce a new behavior with her children. Very clever I thought.

Do not try to initiate change of troublesome behaviors just before Christmas vacation or the annual visit from grandparents. Choose a time that is more stable and predictable. This will give you the time and structure that you need to be consistent.

Be Mindful of the Time of Day

There are three blocks of time each day that correlate to increases in misbehavior. Morning routine is often difficult because of pressure to be out the door and off to work and school. This extra pressure makes parents and children feel tense and urgent. It is a time when tempers erupt and reason and calm abandon us. Prepare for this each day. It is better to awaken everyone 20 minutes earlier to ensure enough time to get ready. Take 10 minutes to have breakfast together and have fun. Relax. Model calmness. This teaches children to get their moods ready for the day.

Research has shown that the most difficult time of day for parents and children is the time between after school and dinner. Parents are tired. The children want to release energy that has be stored all day in school. What these studies have concluded is that this is also a time when everyone's blood sugar is low. This makes us irritable. It may be helpful for you and the children to have a snack. It also helps to have a plan for the children. Keep them busy.

Bedtime is a problem for some children. Do not teach your children that going to bed is a punishment that comes at the end of each day. Going to bed is a time to relax and get comfortable. Have a bedtime routine: bath, snack, story, hug and kiss. Use a chart or checklist to teach children to regulate their own bedtime routine. Do not use going to bed early as a punishment. Being sensitive to these difficult times of day helps you focus and be more consistent.

Expect Challenge

Children will test you. No matter how carefully you plan or how strongly committed, your children will resist change. Children often respond well to new discipline techniques at first. After a while, they drift back to previous patterns. Misbehaviors increase. When this happens, do not despair. This is normal. Once you realize that occasional testing of limits will occur, you will be less frustrated and disappointed. Knowing this helps you be more consistent during these periods.

Make the Commitment

The seventh strategy that helps you be more consistent is the awareness that consistency is one of the most important factors in successful parenting. Consistency teaches children what to expect. It teaches children how to predict the consequences of their actions. Once a child can predict the outcome of his behavior, he will make better choices. Making better choices is the key to developing responsibility.

Understanding the importance of consistency will make you more consistent. Consistency is important when teaching positive behaviors. The more consistently you use positive feedback, the more quickly your child will learn appropriate behaviors. This is especially true when you are trying to teach new priority behaviors. Every time you find your children playing nicely, thank them for being cooperative. When you see your son making an effort to clean his room, mention how proud you feel. Explain how he is growing up and becoming responsible. He is helping the whole family.

Consistency is important when you use punishment. Once you tell your child that a misbehavior will be punished, always follow through. If you slip up or only use punishment when you feel like it, you will make the problem worse. You will teach your child that you do not mean what you say. You will teach your child to be persistent in a negative way. You will teach your child that sooner or later he will get away with misbehaving.

Consistency is an expression of love and caring. When you behave consistently, your children will have better self-discipline. They will see that they are important to you. "I know my parents care about me because they put in the energy and time to make sure that I behave." When you behave consistently, you are telling your children that you will do whatever it takes. That's your job. Children seldom verbalize that they prefer parents who follow through, but they do. It is especially important to teenagers.

Inconsistency causes children to be unsure of themselves. It makes children feel unimportant, insecure and confused. This confusion compels children to manipulate, tease, or take advantage of unclear situations. Once your children learn that you mean what you say and you are consistent, they will take you more seriously. They will think more carefully about all their behaviors and decisions. Thinking is what you want.

The next time that you feel you need a vacation from consistency, remember Mrs. Ellis. Think about the consequences. Misbehaviors will get worse and they will happen more frequently. Inconsistency teaches children that you do not mean what you say. Once your child learns this, he will try to get away with other misbehaviors. "If I can get away with skipping my chores, let's see what happens when I come home late." This creates a cycle where children become increasingly persistent in a negative way. Consistency breaks this cycle.

A certain amount of misbehavior is normal in all children. When you respond to misbehavior consistently, the misbehavior will decrease. When you respond to misbehavior inconsistently, the misbehavior will increase.

Summary

Consistency is most important, yet it is difficult to do. Reward yourself after you have persisted through a difficult situation. Use your energy wisely. Focus on priority behaviors. Use signs to give yourself reminders. Be mindful of time of day. Expect challenges. Remember that consistency is an expression of love and caring. It tells your children they are important. Be patient. Change takes time.

Part IV: HOW TO MANAGE MISBEHAVIOR

Chapter 14

How Children Learn To Misbehave

"Please do the dishes, Paul."
"I don't feel like it now."
"Paul, it's your turn to do the dishes."
"Can't I do them later?"
"It's time now, Paul, please."
"I don't want to do the dishes tonight."
"Do the dishes and I'll give you a dollar."
"Make it two dollars and you've got a deal."

This parent is offering a reward to a child who is arguing and trying to avoid doing his job. *A bribe is reward for misbehavior*. A bribe is an attempt to coax a misbehaving child into good behavior.

Bribery makes children obnoxious. Bribery places power in the hands of your children. Do not use bribes to persuade your child to change his mind. When you bribe a child, you are encouraging him to be disagreeable in the future. "I refused to do the dishes. Now I am two dollars richer." If a child misbehaves, deal with it. Do not be tempted by bribery.

When Michael had a tantrum in the supermarket, Connie bribed him into being quiet by giving him a candy bar. She rewarded him for teasing and whining. Although she got a quiet child, Connie will get a tantrum every time she takes Michael shopping. By rewarding his tantrum, Michael learns that *tantrums get him what he wants*. This is how misbehavior patterns are developed.

Many reasonable and well meaning parents have accidentally or unintentionally taught their children to misbehave. Connie never intended to teach Michael to have tantrums. If you would ask her if she were teaching Michael to misbehave, she would be appalled. "Are you joking? I have worked my head off trying to get him to mind."

Some parents begin rewarding unacceptable behavior while their children are quite young. Consider the parent who uses a treat to comfort an unhappy child. The treat will probably coax the child into a better mood. The youngster may learn that one way to get a treat is to act unhappy. Unhappiness is rewarded. The child associates unhappiness with food. Whenever something unpleasant occurs, food will make the hurt go away.

Some circumstances in life are unpleasant. We need to face these events without a Twinkie on our lips. This connection between food and discomfort in childhood often results in poor eating habits in adulthood. Think about sitting around the house with nothing to do. How many times do you look in the refrigerator?

Whining, Teasing and Tantrums

Children whine, tease and have tantrums to get their way. Children are experts at manipulating their parents. Some of it, they come by naturally. Some of it, we teach them. Giving in to tantrums and other demands causes these misbehaviors to increase in the future. Often, we establish this pattern by the time a child is two years old.

Almost every time you go shopping, you see a child like Michael. You may have been humbled yourself a few times. I have been. Before I became a parent, I used to wonder how children got away with this. Now it's clear. It's easy to give in.

When a child gets what he wants by having an outburst, he learns there is a pay-off for misbehaving. Once learned, this pattern is difficult to change. You change it by not giving in. Stop the pay-off.

Extinction

A behavior that is not rewarded will not recur. This is called extinction. Behaviors that are not paid off will stop happening. Extinction means you must eliminate rewards that follows a child's misbehavior. You must eliminate the pay-offs that encourage more misbehavior in the future. Extinction means that Connie must stop giving Michael a candy bar. She must stop no matter how embarrassing his tantrum becomes.

With parental persistence and consistency, tantrums and demands that are not rewarded will eventually disappear. The key word is eventually. Behavior change takes time. (Remember reading about patience in Chapter 1?) In many cases, tantrums will get worse before they get better. Consider the child's point of view. "I usually get what I want by having a tantrum. Now my Mom is ignoring my tantrums. I'll get her attention this time. I'll show her a tantrum she will never forget."

It is not uncommon for tantrums and demanding misbehavior to intensify for a brief period when you stop giving in to them. This increase is called an extinction burst. Children who are persistent have greater tantrums at first. The more a child has been rewarded, the more the misbehavior will resist extinction.

Once you decide to stop giving in, you must do so forever. Never give in again. Imagine what would happen. Connie decides that she will not give in to Michael's tantrum. She will not buy him the candy he demands. Off they go to the supermarket. By aisle 3, Michael is having a tantrum. Connie hangs in there. Michael's face is getting red. So is Connie's. Aisle 5 — they have never made it this far without the candy. Michael is yelling and screaming and kicking. The situation has never been this bad. Connie's knees are getting weak. So is her will. Aisle 7 — Michael is in a frenzy. Connie holds out and holds out and holds out. As Michael is about to launch a jar of raspberry preserves at an astonished bystander, Connie's will crumbles. She gives in. Everyone is calm as Michael eats his candy bar quietly on aisle 9.

Connie has just taught Michael to have bigger tantrums and be more persistent. Once you decide to stop giving in, you must do so always. Even when you are tired. Even when you do not feel like being consistent. Even when you have had a long miserable day. If you start to use extinction and then give in, you will make the misbehavior worse. If you give in to bigger tantrums and demands, you will be rewarding bigger tantrums and demands. You will get longer and louder tantrums in the future.

Be consistent. Follow through. Once you say it, do it. If you do not think you can outlast the extinction burst, then do not start. Wait until you have the courage and the energy. You will need support from your spouse. It is important to work together. It will emphasize the point to your child that you both mean business. If your spouse will not cooperate, be consistent anyway. It will take a little longer for your efforts to show results. Your child will learn that you mean what you say. He will behave better for you. He will behave as always for your spouse.

Be patient. Most parents fail because they lack patience. You must be more persistent than your child. If you give in, you lose. You must control yourself. Do not yell. Do not lose your temper. That will only make matters worse. Your reward will be well-behaved children.

If you have a bad day, put it behind you. If you give in, do not dwell on it. If you are short on patience, regain your balance. Being patient and consistent is not easy. If you slip back into old habits, do not criticize yourself. Start fresh. Think of the future.

You Can Not Eliminate Some Pay-offs

Extinction weakens misbehaviors that are demanding or attention getting. Extinction will not improve all misbehaviors because there are some rewards for misbehavior that you cannot eliminate. There are other reasons why children misbehave. Consider the teenager who smokes cigarettes. You can forbid smoking in the house. You can throw away the cigarettes when you find them. You can even punish the youngster. These sanctions may help curtail the smoking.

However, there are pay-offs operating that you cannot control. You cannot control peer pressure. His friends encourage smoking. He earns social status by smoking. Smoking is what everyone else is doing. You cannot eliminate all the rewards for smoking. Therefore, despite your efforts, smoking will continue.

Extinction Works Both Ways

Extinction weakens misbehaviors. It also weakens good behaviors that are not reinforced. When positive behaviors are ignored, they may be replaced by misbehavior. "Why be good? It's not worth it." Use positive feedback when your children are behaving. Do not ignore good behavior. Focus on what your children are doing right. Catch your children being good.

Do Not Make Excuses

Some children misbehave because parents make excuses. "He is just tired." "She has had a long day." "He has not eaten." "She always acts that way when he is around." Sometimes we teach our children to misbehave by making excuses for them.

When you make excuses, you are implying that your child is not capable of behaving. Excuses teach children they do not have to be responsible for their behavior. You are teaching them that misbehavior is justified as long as you can come up with a good reason. Making excuses will come back to haunt you. When you make excuses, you are giving your children reasons to misbehave in the future. They will use these excuses to argue and avoid responsibility.

Many teenagers were taught to be irresponsible by their parents. When these teenagers were younger and still impressionable, their parents made excuses for them. Many parents believe that making excuses is the proper thing for a parent to do. It is not.

Never Ask "Why?"

One way to avoid buying into excuses and teach responsibility at the same time is to avoid asking *why*. The question *why* asks for an excuse. The question *what* does not. Rather than ask *why*, ask *what*. Asking *why* usually leads to long arguments or debates. Asking *what* helps your child focus on the misbehavior. Here is how this works. Instead of asking a question such as "Why did you do that?", ask your child "What did you do?" The purpose of asking the "what" question is to avoid the excuses and have your child simply tell you what happened. Some children resist this at first. They are in the habit of answering "why" questions. Do not let them tell you "why" they did it. What you need to do now is help the youngster describe what he did. So if your child tries to tell you why he did it, stop him. Say "I didn't ask you why you did it. I asked you to tell me what you did." Once you get your child to describe what he did, talk about correct behavior. "What could you have done so you would not be in trouble now?" This approach avoids making excuses. There is more about this strategy in Chapter 22.

Summary

We are tempted to bribe children into behaving because there is a temporary pay-off. We like quick solutions. Bribery teaches children to be more argumentative and oppositional. Bribery encourages more misbehavior. Do not reward unacceptable behavior. Do not give in to demands, whining or teasing. Stop the pay-off permanently. Be consistent and patient.

Do not make excuses. When a child misbehaves, deal with it — always. Excuses give children reasons to misbehave.

Chapter 15

Why Children Push Your Button

It's 10:10 and thirteen-year-old Megan is still on the telephone. The rule is, there will be no telephone conversations after 10 o'clock. Mother sticks her head into Megan's room and politely reminds her that she needs to finish the conversation and hang up. Megan nods and makes a face. At 10:20, Mother calmly reminds her again. Megan waves at Mom hoping she will go away. This time Mother feels herself getting upset. At 10:27, Mother explodes with anger. "Hang up right now young lady. You are restricted from the phone for two weeks." Megan has pushed Mother's button.

Children push your button because they like driving you crazy. They like seeing you transformed from a rational, clearheaded, calm parent into an unreasonable, provoked maniac. One minute you are composed and sensible. The next minute you are agitated and senseless.

Every parent can relate to this. When you get angry, yell, scream, or threaten, your button has been pushed. When you find yourself telling your child that he is grounded for a year, your button has been pushed.

Children push your button hoping you will give in and let them have their way. Children push your button to get attention. Children push your button because they want you to feel guilty and blame yourself when you punish them. Children push your button because they are angry at you. Some children push your button to get even and hurt you.

We all have this button. When it is pushed, each of us reacts in our own unique way. Usually, we become angry, impulsive, and sometimes vengeful.

Two Reactions for One Misbehavior

Twelve-year-old Sean asks his mother, Cindy, if he can have a few friends over to watch TV. Cindy says "no." She explains that she has a lot of work to do tonight. "Perhaps you can have them over some other night. Maybe next weekend." Sean does not accept her answer. He begins to tease and whine. "I never get to have friends over. You're not fair." Cindy argues her point. Sean argues in return. The argument intensifies. Sean starts having a tantrum. Cindy gets angry. She yells at Sean to go to his room and stay there for the remainder of the day.

Going to his room is a punishment. Arguing should be weakened. In reality, Sean is arguing more every day. Even though Cindy consistently sends Sean to his room every time, Sean continues to argue.

Sean argues to push Cindy's button. Cindy had two reactions to Sean's misbehavior. She became angry with Sean. She punished Sean. What if making Cindy angry was part of Sean's plan? What if Cindy's anger was a payoff for Sean? Then Cindy's anger was a reward.

When Cindy punishes Sean for arguing, she concurrently rewards him for arguing. Sean trades going to his room for making Cindy upset. This gives Sean control and power. That is why Sean continues to argue each day even though Cindy punishes him consistently. *The reward of control is stronger than the punishment.* Cindy must change her behavior. She must learn to control her anger when she punishes Sean. She must stay calm and not argue. By controlling herself, Cindy removes Sean's reward for arguing, therefore, the punishment will have more of an effect.

When some parents learn this, they respond by wanting to use stronger punishments. Large punishments combined with anger could be disastrous. Even if you use a punishment that is stronger than the reward of pushing your button, your anger greatly neutralizes the effects of the punishment. It will take much longer for the punishment to weaken the misbehavior.

How to Cope with Anger, Stress and Guilt

Guilt, anger, stress, fear, anxiety and most other unpleasant emotions are self-defeating. Anger impairs your judgment. It rewards a power seeking child. Guilt makes you compensate. You do not follow through. You feel sorry for not being a perfect parent and you try to make it up to your child by giving in.

These feelings interfere with successful parenting. They inhibit your relationship with your children. They can cause misbehavior to increase. Learning how to cope with self-defeating emotions and beliefs will increase your happiness as a person, a spouse, and a parent.

If you want to reduce the amount of negative emotions in your life, you must believe two things. You control your thoughts. Your thoughts control your emotions. Therefore, you control how you feel. You control happiness, joy and excitement. You control guilt, anger, stress, and fear.

I lived many years believing that unsafe drivers, poorly planned freeways, dead car batteries and uncapped toothpaste made me angry. I used to believe that untrained sales clerks and incompetent waitresses made me angry. I now realize that these circumstances are part of life. I can choose to be angry or stay calm. I prefer staying calm. I allow much less anger in my life than I did ten years ago. I still get angry. When I do, I realize what has happened and I let it go.

I once felt guilty for not having all the answers and failing to meet the needs of every parent and child that came to me for help. I now accept my humanness and imperfection. It is easy to succumb to self-defeating behaviors. Resisting them takes practice.

You will always be tempted to give in to self-defeating emotions. You will have spontaneous reactions that seem impossible to control. You might still feel guilty and angry when your child has a tantrum in public. You become discouraged if your son gets a failing report card. However, you can do a lot to improve your day-to-day experience. A certain amount of child misbehavior and aggravation is part of parenting. Children can create frustration and discouragement. Their misbehavior can push your button. If your children push your button, take preventive action. Make a plan to protect yourself.

Defending Yourself Against Button Attacks

Some parents find it helpful to have a technique that diffuses their anger. Go sit in your room for a few minutes. Listen to music. Go for a walk. Count to 25. Think peaceful thoughts. Reward yourself when you do survive a button attack.

Do not expect perfection from yourself the first week. Make your goal more realistic. If you have an episode where one of your children successfully pushes your button, do not put yourself down. Do not think that you are a failure. You are human. Do not let your disappointment keep you down. Encourage yourself just as you would encourage one of your children. Do not dwell on your inadequacies. Focus on the times that you were able to maintain your control in frustrating situations. Think about the times you were successful.

Your button has an important influence on the way you discipline your children. Conflicts can be resolved without anger. Stay calm. Your communication is more effective. Punishment is more effective. You present yourself as a model for self-control. Your children learn more effectively.

You may have to protect your button for weeks before you see results. Your children will test you. That's how it works. Even though you are not getting angry anymore, your children will still test you. They will still try to push your button. Do not give in to their attacks.

What happens if you do give in occasionally? What happens if you still get angry once in a while? You will probably make the problem worse. You will be encouraging your children to push your button more, not less. That's why it is so important to protect your button. Be strong. Be consistent.

How to Express Anger Constructively

There will be times when you get angry. Occasional anger is normal. Do not feel guilty about it. It is okay for your children to know that you have a boiling point. It is not okay to let your anger get in the way of good discipline.

Many parents get angry but do not say or do anything about it. Most parents save anger. This is a mistake. This is the San Andreas syndrome. Pressure builds and builds and then the earth quakes. We let our anger build and build until we crack. This confuses children. "I have had two other fights with my brother today. This time Mom acts as though we killed somebody." Do not save anger. When you save anger, it can become uncontrollable.

Let it out slowly and in small amounts. Tell your child what he did, how you feel and why you feel that way. "When you fight like that, I get angry because you could get hurt or break something." "When you don't call home, I get worried that something might have happened to you."

Summary

Children push your button to get a reaction. They hope you will get upset and change your mind or give in. Do not let your emotions get the best of you. Deal with misbehaviors as they happen. This helps you vent without blame. This keeps you from saving anger and then exploding. It is better for your mental health. It is better for your children.

What Are Your Button Pushers?

Make a list of the misbehaviors that push your button. What misbehaviors get you angry and upset? Next, outline a plan to deal with each button pusher.

Example:
Button Pusher: Your two children argue.

Plan: Stay calm — do not get angry or yell.
        If I get angry, go sit in my room.
        Cool off before I say anything.
        Let it out slowly.
        Do not save your anger until it erupts.
        "I feel angry when you argue like that."
        Spotlight the positive — focus on cooperation.
        Look for times when they agree.

Button Pusher: _____

Plan: _____

_____

_____

Button Pusher: _____

Plan: _____

_____

_____

Chapter 16

Use Punishments That Teach

At Brandt and Audra's house, beds need to be made before leaving for school. If you fail to make your bed, you go to bed thirty minutes early. The last time that Brandt failed to make his bed was three weeks ago. Audra fails to make her bed about four mornings a week. She goes to bed early each time.

Most parents believe that going to bed early is a good punishment. This seems like a good plan. Look at what is actually happening. This form of punishment works well for Brandt. He avoids the punishment by remembering to make his bed. He has decided that staying up a little later is important.

Going to bed early is not a punishment for Audra. She does not avoid it. Going to bed early has had no effect on her behavior. She is not making her bed. Maybe she likes going to bed early. I certainly do! This punishment works well for Brandt. It does not work for Audra. Another punishment should be used for Audra. Something that will change her behavior.

Punishment is a negative consequence. When used properly, punishment eliminates or reduces misbehavior. Using punishment correctly is difficult. It requires consistent follow-through. Too much punishment is harmful. It creates unpleasant feelings. It drains energy. Punishment works, but it is not easy to use effectively. Most parents believe that punishing a misbehavior will stop the child from repeating the misbehavior. Sometimes this is true. Sometimes it is not.

"How do you punish your children?"

"I yell."

"How do your children react to your yelling?"

"They don't react. They usually ignore me."

"Then what?"

"I get angry. Sometimes I yell again."

"Do they stop?"

"For a while, maybe."

"What do you try next?"

"Sometimes I spank them."

"How often do you have to spank them?"

"About eight or ten times a day."

Any punishment that is used this often is not working. The misbehavior is not getting better. The children are not listening to the yelling. They are not avoiding the spankings.

Good Punishments Are Seldom Used

A true punishment is one that is seldom used because it is seldom needed. This is punishment's golden rule. Punishment should reduce the need for more punishment. Punishment should decrease the misbehavior. If the misbehavior does not change, then the punishment is not working. Many parents make this mistake. Many parents focus on the punishment rather than the misbehavior. If you punish your child five or six times a day for the same misbehavior, the punishment is not working. If you keep adding to the punishment and the misbehavior continues, the punishment is not working. It is not the punishment that is important, it is the misbehavior that is important. A punishment must change the misbehavior. If it doesn't, try something else. You may think that yelling, threatening, scolding and spanking are good punishments. These reactions release your anger. They are not good punishments. They have little long-term effect on misbehavior. Anger and punishment do not mix.

Do Not Punish When You Are Angry

Linda hurried home one day to take her dog to the vet. When she arrived home, she heard someone in the house. She was ready to run next door and call the police when she heard a giggle. She called out. There was another giggle. She went into her thirteen-year-old daughter's bedroom. Another giggle. Nancie and two friends were hiding in the closet. They were skipping school. Linda was so angry she could not think straight. All she could say was, "Nancie, it's going to take me and your father a few days to think about how you will be punished for this." Linda did not let her anger get in the way of being rational and making a good judgment. Allowing her daughter to worry for a few days is a pretty good punishment all by itself.

Whenever I do a workshop on punishment, I explain this next point carefully. For many parents, this is an idea with considerable impact. When you punish in anger, you are actually doing two things at the same time. You are punishing. You are reacting with anger. What if your child intended to get you angry? What if your child wanted to get even or retaliate because of something that happened earlier? Seeing you get angry is not a punishment. *It is a reward!* When you get angry at a misbehavior, you are teaching your child how to have control over your emotional state of mind. You are giving your child power over you. This is a pay-off. The misbehavior is reinforced, not punished. As a result, the misbehavior increases. The effects of the punishment are negated by the reward of getting you angry. Some children would trade a swat on the bottom for the power they receive when they have succeeded in getting you angry. The only way to break this cycle of retaliation is to stop punishing with anger. If you find yourself getting angry, walk away. Dispense with your anger first, then confront the misbehavior. Do not let your children push your button.

Do not punish when you are angry. Cool off first. The purpose of punishment is to teach your children to behave better in the future. The purpose is not to get even. Sometimes your children can make you very angry but this is not the time to hand out punishment. I remember a child who was upset because he was grounded forever. When I spoke with his dad, he explained that the boy had lost some of his tools. He got so angry at his son he grounded him for the rest of his life. He overreacted.

When you overreact because you are angry, you may say things that you do not mean. You cannot ground a child for life. Do not punish when you are angry. You will be teaching your children that punishment is a form of revenge.

The purpose of punishment is to change a misbehavior and teach better decision-making. Punishment is most effective when it is predetermined and planned. Punishment does not work well as an impulsive reaction. When you become angry, you are acting as a model for negative behavior. You will not be teaching your children to make better decisions.

Do Not Punish To Embarrass

Punishment should not embarrass, humiliate or degrade children. Punishment is meant to teach your child that misbehaving is not a good decision and behaving is a good decision. When punishment embarrasses your child, it creates unhealthy feelings. The embarrassment will only cause your child to think of you as mean or unfair. When this occurs, your child will not learn to make better decisions. He will not learn cooperation. Your child may strike back in anger. This can start a negative cycle.

Do not punish your child in front of other children. Take your child aside. Tell him what he has done and that he will be punished. Talk about it later, when the two of you are alone.

Use Punishment Consistently

Punishment must be administered consistently. Once you decide to punish a misbehavior, do so always. If you punish only when you feel like it, you will make the problem worse. Once you tell your child that he is going to be punished, follow through. You must use punishment consistently, even after you have had a long, miserable day. You can never miss or let the misbehavior slide. Not even once. Many parents make this mistake. Children love it. It motivates them to test you — to see if you will punish them this time.

Angela wanted to know why punishment did not have any effect on her son, Bryan. She explained that she "tried everything. Nothing bothers him. He never does what I ask him to do." After more discussion, I learned that Angela punishes Brian once or twice a week. He does what he pleases all the other times. Angela does not follow through consistently. Bryan can misbehave several times a day and only be punished once or twice a week. This is a trade-off most children would make gladly. Angela and Bryan were trapped in a pattern. She did not punish consistently because she believed it did not work. He continued to misbehave because he got away with it most of the time. He was not punished consistently. Angela worked out a plan that used positive feedback and punishment. She emphasized cooperation and good decisions. She used small punishments, but she used them consistently. As Angela's behavior improved, Bryan's behavior improved.

Be Reasonable

Punishment must be reasonable. Short and simple punishments are more effective than harsh punishments. React appropriately to the size of the misbehavior. Do not restrict your son for a month because he did not finish his vegetables. Take away his dessert. When punishments are reasonable, children learn what behaviors are important.

Punishment should be administered as soon after the misbehavior as possible. The more immediate, the more effective the punishment will be. This is especially true with young children. The only exception to this rule occurs when you are angry. Do not punish immediately when you are angry. Wait until you settle down, just as Linda did when she caught Nancie skipping school. You might say, "You will be punished for this, but I have to cool down first."

With misbehaviors that are recurrent, punishment should only be used after you have tried several positive remedies. Most adults think of punishment first. Most adults think that you always treat a misbehavior with a punishment. You can improve misbehavior by using positive feedback to strengthen the opposite of the misbehavior. Your two children argue constantly. "If you do not stop fighting you will both be grounded for the weekend." Point out the opposite rather than punish. The opposite of arguing is cooperating. Use encouragement and positive feedback when they are cooperating and sharing. "It's good to see you having fun. You should be proud of yourselves for the way you are sharing the computer." Immediately resorting

130

to punishment traps many parents. No one likes how it feels.
One way to escape this trap is to focus on positive behavior.

Your Turn

Pam cannot understand why Steven will not behave.
Pam wants to be more positive but sometimes forgets. Steven
is a very active child. He gets into things he is not supposed to
touch. Whenever Steven does not mind, Pam becomes upset
and frustrated. Pam yells a lot. She spanks too. Nothing seems
to work. What can you tell Pam about her behavior?

Summary

Pam needs to realize that her style of punishment is
not working. Steven has become immune to the yelling and
the spanking. His misbehavior is not improving. Pam needs to
control herself. Getting angry and frustrated is only aggravat-
ing the situation. Her anger may be rewarding to Steven. Most
of all, Pam must remember to be positive. The strongest tool
she has is positive feedback.

Punishment works, but it is not easy to use. Positive feedback is much easier to use and more fun to use.
Positive feedback creates internal motivation in children.
It teaches self-discipline and promotes a healthy and pleasant family climate. Successful parents emphasize the positive. Positive feedback, extinction and punishment are always in effect, whether you are conscious of them or not.
The key to successful parenting is to be aware of these
principles and use them to your advantage.

Parents who are only interested in controlling misbehavior will punish. Parents who want children to be
cooperative will balance positive feedback with extinction and
redirection and use a minimal amount of punishment. If you
emphasize the positive, you will only need a minimal amount
of punishment.

The next four pages are refrigerator pages — make a photocopy and hang them on the refrigerator. The first page is a list of questions to ask yourself about the way you use punishment. The second page is a summary of strategies that strengthen or weaken behavior. The next two pages are a comparison between positive feedback and punishment. Many parents have told me that an occasional review of these pages helps them keep a positive focus. I hope they do the same for you.

Here are ten questions to ask when you use punishment.

1. Will this punishment teach my child better decision-making skills?

2. Does this punishment change the misbehavior?

3. Does this punishment reduce the need for more punishment?

4. Am I getting angry when I punish?

5.Is this punishment part of a plan? Do I use it impulsively?

6. Am I getting even? Will this punishment humiliate or embarrass my child?

7. Am I being consistent?

8. Will I follow through immediately (except when I am angry)?

9. Is this punishment reasonable and fair?

10. Have I tried positive remedies first?

How To Strengthen Or Weaken Behavior

To strengthen a good behavior:
Use positive feedback.
<u>Examples:</u>
When your children behave, reward them by thanking them. When you see your children sharing, tell them that they should be proud of themselves.

To reduce misbehavior:
1. Use positive feedback to strengthen the opposite behavior.
<u>Examples:</u>
If you want to reduce the amount of arguing between two children, call attention to the time when they are not arguing.
If your children have a negative attitude, reward anything positive.

2. Use extinction to eliminate any rewards for misbehavior.
<u>Examples:</u>
Do not give in to your children's demands.
Ignore your children when they try to get your attention in a negative way.

3. Use punishment.
<u>Examples:</u>
A child who comes home late cannot go out the next day. A child who does not do his chores forfeits part of his allowance.

A Comparison Between
Positive Feedback and Punishment

Positive Feedback feels good to give and receive.	Punishment creates unpleasant feelings, often anger.
Positive Feedback emphasizes good behavior. It teaches children to think.	Punishment draws attention to misbehavior.
Positive Feedback increases motivation.	Punishment can have a negative effect on motivation.
Positive Feedback creates feelings of success.	Punishment can cause children to feel like failures.
Positive Feedback improves a child's self-esteem.	Punishment can have a negative impact on self-esteem.
Positive Feedback gives children self confidence.	Punishment weakens self-confidence.
Positive Feedback teaches children to trust their decisions.	Punishment does not teach trust. It sometimes teaches fear.

Positive Feedback motivates children to seek goals.	Punishment may cause children to feel despair. "Why try? I always get in trouble anyway."
Positive Feedback develops responsibility. "When I make good decisions, I feel good."	Punishment often teaches children to avoid admitting responsibility for their actions.
Positive Feedback promotes healthy family relationships.	Punishment may alienate family members.
Positive Feedback encourages children to talk to their parents.	Punishment discourages children from talking to their parents.
Positive Feedback teaches children to be positive with others.	Punishment that is aggressive teaches children to be aggressive towards others.
Positive Feedback is easy to use effectively.	Punishment is difficult to use easily.

136

Chapter 17

How To Punish Your Children
Without Punishing Yourself

It was late in the afternoon on July 4th. We had planned to go to the evening fireworks display. Our children were arguing more than usual. I threatened them, hoping they would stop. "If you don't quit arguing, we are not going to the fireworks." What a foolish thing to say. If they did not go, we did not go. There was no way we would have found a baby-sitter at 5:00 P.M. on the Fourth of July. Every teenager in town was going to the fireworks. They did not stop and we did not go. We were punished along with our children.

A better punishment would have been to separate them when they started arguing. Make them play alone. I did not think. I got angry and made a foolish threat that ended up costing me more than my children. Think carefully before talking. Anger can get you in trouble. Think about how the punishment will affect you and the rest of the family. Will this punishment disrupt me? If you have a child who likes to control you or others in the family, choose his punishments carefully. Be sure that the punishment only affects your child who misbehaved and not anyone else. Do not say, "We are not going until you clean your room." If you are going somewhere he wants to go, this threat may work. If he does not want to go, you have just given your child a lot of power. No one can go until the room is clean. You are giving this child control over the entire family. Who is being punished?

What do you do with your child who is not permitted to go somewhere with the rest of the family? Get a baby-sitter and then go and have a good time. You may want to have your child pay for some or all the cost of the baby-sitter. Your child will learn that his misbehavior will not prevent the family from having fun. Select punishments that impact your child, not you. Your other children will learn something too. Misbehavior only affects the one who misbehaves.

Parents often wonder how to take TV privileges from one child. If they have to shut off the TV, the other children will be punished. That's true. Do not shut the TV off because one child is restricted. That punishes everyone. Watch TV as usual. The child who is being punished has to go in another room. That's the true punishment. If no one can watch TV because he cannot watch TV, you are giving your child control over the entire family. Who is being punished?

Use Punishments that are Easy to Enforce

Choose punishments that you can enforce easily. This will enable you to follow through. If a punishment is inconvenient or laborious, you will be less consistent. A father told me that he would lock up the video game for three hours whenever his son would disobey.

"How often do you lock up the game?"

"Once or twice a week."

"Does your son obey all the other days?"

"If he did, would I be talking with you?"

"Why don't you lock up the game every time he disobeys?"

"If I locked that game up every time he did not do what he was supposed to do, I would be locking that thing up ten times a day."

138

"Why don't you do that?"

"It would take me forever with all those
cables and plugs."

Dad is using a punishment that is inconvenient.
Dad does not follow through consistently. His son is not
learning to obey. His son is learning that he can disobey as
often as he likes and only lose his game once or twice a
week. Dad has probably identified an effective punishment
— taking away the video game. Dad needs to be more
consistent. He needs to lock up the game every time. If
the video game cables make this punishment cumbersome,
then Dad needs a more effective way of administering the
punishment.

Explain the Punishment

Tell your child the purpose of the punishment.
When you explain punishment you increase your child's
understanding and cooperation. Explain that you are on
his side. You are not the enemy. You are trying to help
him make better decisions in the future.

"I am not trying to hurt you or make
you angry. You are being punished because
you made a poor choice about your behavior. I want you to learn from this so
you will think differently next time. I do
not want you to think I am out to get you.
I am not. I am out to help you."

Explain that you are not trying to get even. Ignore
irritating comments such as, "You expect me to believe
you are doing this for me. Sure you are." Only explain it
once. Do not become caught in lengthy explanations and
arguments.

Use Punishments that are Realistic

Select punishments that fit the crime. Use reality consequences. A child who makes a mess cleans the mess. A child who pees in the refrigerator should clean the refrigerator. A child who carelessly breaks something should fix it or work to pay for it. A child who comes home late should not go out the next day. A child who does not put his dirty clothes in the laundry basket does his own wash. Children who can operate CD players, VCR's and computers can operate a washing machine. These examples illustrate consequences that are relevant to the misbehavior. They have more meaning to your child. They help teach a lesson.

Some children can be trusted to choose their punishment. This helps them learn more quickly. It shows them that you want to be fair. It encourages them to be mature and responsible.

> "Your behavior has been very good until this incident. I am going to trust you to choose your own punishment for this misbehavior. I know you will be fair and just. Let me know what you decide."

Bigger Does Not Mean Better

Mild punishments are usually more productive than harsh punishments. Keep things in perspective. Don't bring out a cannon to get your children to hang up the towels. Punishments that are short and sweet teach better lessons. Large punishments often create feelings of anger or revenge. When your child feels angry, little learning takes place. When your child believes that you have been unjust in your use of punishment, your child often retaliates or argues. This can start a negative cycle. You punish, your child becomes angry and retaliates by misbehaving again, maybe worse than before. You punish again, perhaps a little more severely, just to make your point. Your child becomes more angry and retaliates by misbehaving again. I have worked with families where the parents were punishing their children for things that happened months ago.

"How long have you been grounded?"

"Since the beginning of last semester."

"How long is that?"

"About five months."

"What are you grounded from?"

"Everything. No dates. No friends. No TV. No phone calls. No stereo. No anything. My parents want me to sit in my room every night and study."

"Is that what you do?"

"I sneak out my window after they go to bed."

"What did you do to get your parents so upset they would ground you for five months?"

"They didn't ground me for five months at first."

"What do you mean?"

"It started with no phone calls for a month."

"What happened?"

"I didn't think it was fair. So I used the phone when they weren't around."

"And...?"

"And I got caught."

"So then your parents made it longer."

"They made it two months and added no friends over."

"Did you think that was fair?"

"Just for using the phone! That wasn't fair

in the first place."
"I think I know the rest."
"It just kept getting worse and worse."
"Was it worth being grounded most of your Sophomore year?"
"Well — no. But I'm not giving up now."

Using Restriction Constructively

Restriction is a useful punishment for children and adolescents. Being grounded is a type of restriction. Restriction means loss of one or more privileges for a specific length of time. You will have to determine what the privilege should be. Some examples are loss of TV time, going to bed early, being restricted from seeing friends, no telephone, no video games, no toys, etc. Choose a restriction that is easy to enforce and that impacts the offender and no one else.

Restricting children for misbehavior is a popular form of punishment. Unfortunately, few parents use restriction effectively. Most parents begin with a period of time that is too long. As adults, we forget that a week or two can be forever to a child. Long periods of restriction are often the result of an argument, hurt feelings or anger. Long periods of restriction can backfire. They can cause your child to feel persecuted or picked on. This can turn into feelings of revenge and a cycle of retaliation begins.

There is a built-in problem with restriction. Many children who become grounded or restricted feel there is no hope. Without hope, there is little reason to behave. "Why behave? I can't go out for a week anyway." Then the child decides that everyone else should be just as miserable. There is a workable solution to this problem.

If you decide to restrict your child, choose an even number of days. Choose 4, 6, 8, or 12 days, depending on the seriousness of the offense and the age of your child. Twelve days is usually the maximum effective period. Anything longer than twelve days and you run the risk of retaliation. Next, explain that each good day will result in one day taken off the end of the restriction period. Let's assume that you have restricted your child for 6 days, Wednesday through Monday. If your child has a good day on Wednesday, then drop Monday. If Thursday is a good day, then drop Sunday. If things go well on Friday, then drop Saturday. Friday is the last day of restriction. You may want to draw a chart or calendar so your child can cross off days and see his progress.

This technique works extremely well. It lets your child know that you want to be fair, even though you mean business. It also lets your child know that you expect proper behavior even while he is restricted. Being restricted is not a license to be uncooperative. Most of all, this approach gives your child a strong incentive to behave immediately. No sitting around the house being miserable for a week.

The success of this strategy depends on how well you define a good day. Then stick to what you say. It helps a great deal to write down what you require.

Rules for dropping a day:

Do what you are asked.
Speak in a pleasant voice.
Be kind and polite to your sister.

Be sure that a good day is truly a good day. Do not drop a day unless it is deserved. If you drop days too easily, you will be defeating the purpose of this approach. Your child can be restricted and still earn other activities.

For example, your child could be restricted from the telephone and still be earning a contract for a new CD. I have worked with preschool teachers who have modified this technique. They use minute restrictions. When a child misuses a toy, the child is restricted from the toy for 10 minutes. If the child behaves, he can earn the toy back in five minutes.

Summary

Choose punishments that affect your child, not you. Choose punishments that can be administered easily. This will motivate you to be consistent. Select punishments that are relevant to the misbehavior. Mild punishments are more effective. Use restriction appropriately. Do not punish when you are angry. The purpose of punishment is to teach, not get even. Practice these guidelines and you will be able to punish your children without punishing yourself.

Chapter 18

Spanking

"My kids don't listen to anything I say."

"What do you do?"

"I spank them. Even though I know it's wrong. I'm always mad at them and then I get mad at myself. I can't live this way. There must be something else I can do."

About 10% of parents spank their children and see nothing wrong with spanking. About 20% of parents never spank their children. About 70% of parents spank their children but wish they didn't. The last sentence says a lot. Many parents want a better way of punishing their children. Parents want to manage their children's misbehavior without getting angry and without spanking.

Does spanking work? Are there any damaging effects? These questions have no exact answers. Even professionals disagree about the value of spanking. Some people argue that spanking works. Others argue that it does not. No wonder many parents are confused about spanking. Spanking is a form of punishment. Is it an acceptable way to punish children? That is for you to decide. This chapter enables you to evaluate the practice of spanking. The first part of this chapter will explain the risks and pitfalls associated with spanking. The remainder of this chapter presents three ways that parents use spanking along with some precautions.

What Happens When You Spank

A spanking usually stops a child's misbehavior. When the misbehavior stops, the parent feels rewarded and learns that spanking works. A spanking can result in good behavior just as a candy bar can buy peace and quiet in the supermarket. Using candy to quiet a tantrum is a temporary solution. You will be feeding your child a lot of candy to keep quiet in the future. Spanking is a temporary solution.

A child who is spanked will usually settle down and behave. After a while, the child acts up again. The parent spanks again because the spanking seemed to work the first time. The child is good for a while and then misbehaves again. The parent spanks again, and so on. This pattern snares many parents.

This pattern occurs because spanking provides external control of children. It does not encourage children to make responsible decisions. It does not promote internal decision making. It teaches children to behave "or else." Children who are frequently spanked do not learn self-control. An eight-year-old once told me that he could misbehave as long as he wanted. "My Mom spanks me when I have to stop."

Spanking is not a good punishment because it happens in a second or two and it's over. Most children would rather have a swat than lose a special privilege for a few days. The spanking is over quickly and they can be off on new adventures. Many children believe that once they have been spanked everything is okay. "We are even." Spanking causes many children to focus on the punishment rather than on their poor decision.

Problems can arise in families where one parent spanks and the other doesn't. This can cause children to avoid the parent who spanks. This avoidance interferes with normal parent-child development. Children see the parent who does not spank as being unable to manage. The children will continue to misbehave for this parent. Children avoid the parent who spanks. Children see the parent who does not spank as weak. Both parents lose.

Spankings have side effects. Spankings are embarrassing. Embarrassment causes children to get angry or think about retaliation. It seldom teaches children to think about how they could have made a better decision. Spankings can affect a child's attitude. Children who are frequently spanked feel insecure. They do not trust themselves. "If I do the wrong thing, I will be hit." Many children who are spanked have poor self-esteem. Some children withdraw. Others become excitable, overactive and aggressive.

Three Ways Parents Use Spanking

The Impulsive Approach

There are three ways that parents use spanking to punish their children: the impulsive approach; the angry approach; and, the planned approach. The impulsive approach is also known as the "all day long" method. A mother once said, "I spank him and spank him and spank him and he still will not listen." He is not listening because the spankings have become meaningless.

The impulsive approach is more commonly used with younger children. These parents are never too serious about the actual swat. They usually grab the child with one hand and swing with the other. The swat is almost automatic or reflexive. The child hollers and then goes about playing. This is also known as the "Barber Shop Syndrome." You have seen parents spank their children five times or more in the 30 minutes they needed to wait their turn for a hair cut.

Many parents use a technique called slap-the-toddler-on-the-hand. Young children like to experiment. They like to touch things to see what happens. When they touch something they shouldn't, they get slapped. Slaps do not teach. Explain why an object should not be touched and remove the child or the object. Your children copy you. When you slap, they learn to slap.

The impulsive approach has no lasting effect on a child's misbehavior. After being spanked on the butt a few dozen times, the swat becomes meaningless. For these parents, spanking is a continuous reaction. These parents do not know any alternative. They think that spanking is what you are obliged to do when your children misbehave. "That's the only way I can get her to behave." They believe they are doing the proper thing to be good parents.

Do children learn anything from the impulsive approach? Nothing that will teach them to make better decisions. Far too often, the spanking depends on how the parent feels at that given moment. If you are short tempered today, your children get spanked for every little thing they do. If you are feeling more tolerable, your children get away with murder. This inconsistency confuses children. "I did this yesterday and it was okay. Today, I'm getting a spanking." This teaches children to be sneaky. It does not teach them right from wrong. It does not teach them how to make better decisions.

Children who are impulsively and frequently spanked believe that hitting is a normal part of life. So when another child does something they do not like, they hit. This becomes a problem with siblings, at school and with playmates. When children hit each other, they get into trouble. This confuses children. When adults hit, it's okay. When children hit, it's not okay.

Children who are frequently spanked believe that everything they do is wrong. This creates poor self-esteem and a lack of self-confidence. The goal of good discipline is to teach our children to make responsible decisions. Frequent spankings do not promote this. Frequent spankings teach children to have poor self-control. Frequent spankings teach children to behave because of fear. If you do not behave, you are spanked. When the parent is not around to provide external control, the child has no control at all.

The impulsive approach is not an effective punishment because it does not minimize the need for future spankings. It perpetuates the need for spankings. Frequent spankings model negative behavior. They are reactive. They are never planned. Parents who use the impulsive approach seldom use positive remedies to change misbehavior.

The Angry Approach

The second way that parents use spanking is the angry approach. This approach is the most common. It is also the most harmful. When you become angry and spank your child, a number of problems result. You teach your child how to "push your button." This teaches your child that his misbehavior has power over your self-control. Spanking in anger is impulsive. It is always a reaction. When you spank in anger, you could become carried away and may hurt your child.

When you spank in anger, you create intense negative emotions. You create these emotions in yourself, your child and the rest of the family. These emotions can damage your child's self-esteem. Many children begin to fear their parents. They begin to mistrust their parents, which leads to a lack of self-trust.

Spanking in anger teaches children to strike out when they are angry. It teaches children that when they are angry, they do not have to exercise self-control, because you do not show self-control when you are angry. Spanking in anger does not teach children how to make better decisions.

When you spank in anger, you are often vengeful. You let your frustration build until it explodes. Then, you retaliate with revenge, sometimes humiliating and embarrassing your child. Children learn they are a source of frustration to you.

If your anger has you trapped in a pattern of spanking, make a commitment to stop. It will take plenty of self-control and rethinking. It is a habit worth changing.

The Planned Approach

The third way that some parents use spanking is the planned approach. This approach means that you tell your child that certain misbehaviors will result in a swat. For example, "If you use bad language, you will be punished by getting a swat." If your child uses bad language, calmly administer a swat. The key word in the last sentence is "calmly." If you do not stay calm, then you are using the angry approach. The planned approach is also known as, "This hurts me more than it does you."

When you use spanking as part of a total plan, it is more effective than when you use it impulsively. However, consider these factors before you use the planned approach. There is no evidence to show that planned spankings teach children to be more responsible. Planned spankings still model negative behavior. If you allow yourself to spank, you may get angry when you spank. You may use spanking inconsistently because of your mood or because you feel guilty. Inconsistency makes the problem worse. Many parents forget that a plan should include positive solutions. They plan to use a spanking as a punishment, but do not plan positive strategies. They forget that the plan should emphasize the positive and not the negative.

I have never known a professional who approved of the impulsive or angry approach. Some professionals approve of the planned approach. If you are going to take the time and energy to implement a plan, why not develop a plan that is positive. Develop a plan that uses other forms of punishment, such as restriction or time-out.

Summary

You can raise self-disciplined children without spanking. Spanking may be a good release for your anger or frustration, however, spanking is a temporary solution that does not teach responsibility. This chapter presented several reasons why spanking can do more harm than good. If you choose to use spanking, use the planned approach. Use a plan that emphasizes the positive; a plan that enables you to maintain your self-control; a plan that gets results.

Chapter 19

Correcting Misbehavior With Time-Out

Judy was twenty-two but looked much older. She had four children. Her oldest was six. She was five months pregnant. She had no time for herself. There was fatigue in her voice. Her four-year-old son, Randy, was driving her crazy. She was not able to manage his tantrums and demands. With tears of desperation, she told how she spent most of her time. "All I do is yell. He never does anything I ask. He just runs around the house making a mess. I don't have time for my other children because of him. I have to do something before this baby is born." After learning about time-out, Judy knew she had a tool — one that would work.

Judy went home and prepared. Randy began the next morning as usual. He refused to come to the breakfast table. Judy put him in time-out. Judy told him to sit quietly for five minutes. Then he could come out. Randy refused to be quiet. He screamed, yelled, cried, and did everything that an enraged four-year-old child can imagine. He was in time-out for an hour and a half. Judy did not give up. She stayed calm. She was consistent. Finally, he sat quietly for five minutes. He came out and had his breakfast. It was 10 o'clock.

Judy's second battle occurred just after noon. Randy refused to lower the volume on the television when asked. Judy placed him in time-out. His resistance was weaker. His will was not as strong. His tantrum was less violent. He was in time-out for only twenty minutes.

Judy used time-out on several other occasions that first week. It became easier to use each time. She trusted time-out. In return, it gave her confidence. Her son was less defiant. Within two weeks, her son was listening. Judy was managing him without screaming and chasing.

Time-out is effective. It is a replacement for yelling, scolding, threatening, and spanking. Time-out prevents your children from pushing your button. Time-out means placing your child in a dull and boring place for a few minutes. It means time away from the group, time away from the fun. Time-out means time away from anything positive. Being denied activity is a kind of punishment.

Three-year-old Laura was a bedtime procrastinator. Laura began screaming and having a tantrum as soon as Donna mentioned bedtime. Pajamas were wrestled on every night. Nagging followed the pajamas. "Can I have a drink of water?" "Would you read me a story?" "There is something wrong with my pillow." Donna believed that these bedtime battles were not caused by any fears. Laura wanted power and control.

Donna used time-out to get Laura to bed. If Laura argued or began whining, she would go to time-out. If Laura refused to go to bed in any way, she would go to time-out. Donna was consistent. When Laura argued or whined, Donna put her in time-out. Then every five minutes, Donna would ask Laura if she were ready to go to bed. After 15 or 20 minutes of sitting alone, Laura was ready to go to bed. In two weeks, Donna sent me a note. "I am beginning to think of the way I disciplined Laura in two ways, before time-out and after time-out. The difference is fantastic. Bedtime is so easy now. She never gets upset or argues. Even when my older children stay up later than she."

Why does time-out work so well? Time-out works because it gives you a tool to back up what you say. Time-out is a teaching technique. It is a mild punishment that you administer quickly and easily. Time-out works because children do not like it. They will behave to avoid it.

Here is an overview. The first step is to select the right setting. Next, choose one misbehavior that you want to eliminate. Finally, explain time-out to your child. Describe the misbehavior that must stop. Explain that the misbehavior will result in time-out. You will need a timer that sounds a bell or a buzzer. An oven timer works fine, as long as your child can hear it from time-out. It may help to have two timers. One for the child to see and one for you. Explain that yours is the official clock! Each of these steps is explained later in this chapter.

There are other aspects of time-out that you need to understand for time-out to be most effective. Time-out is most useful for children between the ages of two and twelve. With certain cautions, you can use time-out with children who are younger than two years old. You can use time-out with children as old as 14, however it may not be as effective. Reality consequences and restriction are more appropriate punishments for teenagers. These punishments are discussed in other parts of this book.

Use time-out with determination and planning. Do not use it impulsively. Your child must be able to predict time-out. Your child must understand when and how you will use time-out. If you use time-out for arguing, do not send your child to time-out for messing up the family room. Choose a more suitable punishment, such as cleaning the family room or other rooms in the house. Your child needs to understand how time-out will work in advance of its initial use. Never use time-out as a surprise.

Use time-out consistently. Once you have said that time-out will punish a misbehavior, do so always. No exceptions. Do not slack off. Do not give in. Do not make excuses. If you do not follow through, even once, you will make the problem worse. You will be creating more work for yourself in the future.

Remain cool and calm when you use time-out. If you let your child push your button, time-out will not work. If you get angry, time-out will not work. If you find yourself yelling and screaming when you use time-out, it will not work. If your child succeeds in getting you upset, the effects of time-out will be weakened.

If you feel a surge of anger, walk away. Calm down. Then return to the situation. I knew a father who put himself in time-out until he cooled off. He would go for a walk or lie down for a while. He knew that interacting with his children when he was angry always had bad results.

The initial episodes of time-out may be difficult. Some children spend over an hour in time-out on the first few occasions. Early in my career, I worked at a home for boys. A child spent two hours in time-out one day. He had misbehaved. He needed to sit quietly for ten minutes. He chose to yell and scream obscenities for two hours before he sat quietly for ten minutes. We hated to hear this child in such a rage. He had to learn that his tantrums would not work. He had to learn to follow the rules.

Some children really work you over in the beginning. Be prepared, particularly if your child has been getting his way for the last four or eight or ten years. Please be assured that after the first few episodes, time-out gets easier for everyone. There will be a day when your child no longer becomes angry when sent to time-out. There will be a day when you will not need time-out at all.

Time-out must be part of a total plan to improve your children's behavior. Time-out should be a small part of the plan. The larger part of the plan should emphasize the positive aspects of your children's behavior. Focus 90%

of your energy on positive behaviors. Catch your children being good. If you take the positive for granted, improvements in your child's behavior will not occur. If you use time-out to correct misbehavior and forget to reinforce good behavior, time-out will not be effective. Without the positive emphasis, using time-out by itself will not work. It will not make a lasting change. Time-out will become another form of punishment that your child will learn to tolerate.

Choosing the Best Setting for Time-Out

The setting for time-out needs to be boring. Most bedrooms are like recreation centers. Use a bathroom, laundry room, utility room, or spare bedroom. Use a room with light. Whichever room you select, make it dull. You may want to put a chair in the room. Remove all opportunities for self-amusement. Remove all dangerous items and breakable objects. Remove anything that is valuable. For most children, you will only need to follow these precautions for three weeks or less. Once your children have learned the procedures for time-out, you may gradually become more trusting.

Many parents have concerns about placing their child in a separate room with the door closed. This is usually more of a problem for the parent than the child. If you do not feel comfortable with the door being closed, you may try leaving it ajar. The risk here is that your child can get up and peak out, make noises for you to hear, listen to other children having fun, and so on. If your child is willing to comply with time-out with the door ajar, there is no problem. Explain to your child that the door can be left ajar as long as he remains quiet and cooperative. If he begins to act up, the door will be closed. Some parents have used a gate across the bathroom doorway. This is

permissible as long as your child does time-out without manipulating.

Time-out is worth the planning and preparation. The
setting for time-out must be completely safe. Make your time-
out room as child-proof as possible. Remove anything that
might cause harm. Your child must be safe there. Your child
must believe that you are confident about the room being safe.
Eliminate any doubts that make you feel uncomfortable. Your
child may use these doubts against you. "I'm scared. I'm afraid
to be alone in here." Do not let these statements influence you
into letting your child out before the time is up. "There is nothing in the bathroom that will hurt you." It may be helpful to sit
in the time-out room yourself for several minutes. Look around.
Pretend you are an angry child. What could you say or do to
make Mom or Dad never want to put you in time-out again?

You may have to withstand pressure from friends and
relatives. Adults who are unfamiliar with time-out may regard
it as cruel. It's ironic that many parents who see time-out as
mean see nothing wrong with spanking. Do not be influenced
by this. I have never known of a child who suffered emotional
damage from sitting alone for ten minutes.

Many parents use the bathroom for time-out. A spare
bathroom is preferable. Bathrooms are sturdy. There are few
amusements in the bathroom. If you use the bathroom, remember, safety first. Remove all the medicines. Remove all
dangerous items such as razors and electrical appliances. Don't
forget to remove the toilet paper.

Steven used the bathroom for time-out with five-
year-old Lynn. Steven thought he had done everything to
make the bathroom safe and boring. Lynn entertained herself by playing with the water in the toilet bowl. Steven's
remedy was to put a clamp on the toilet lid. A little cre-
ativity goes a long way. Steven found a solution to the

problem. He did not abandon the whole idea of time-out just because there was a set-back. He did not say what many parents might have said. "She is just having fun. Time-out doesn't work." He worked through the problem. He was committed to making time-out work.

There is one caution about the bathroom. Do not use the bathroom as your time-out setting for a child who is being toilet trained. This would be confusing. Do not use the bathroom for time-out with any child when another child is being toilet trained. You do not want your toddler to perceive the bathroom as a bad place. Use a utility room or spare bedroom. Use your bedroom as a last resort.

Do not use a chair in the corner or a chair in the hall. Your child will learn that squirming, making faces, rocking, singing, humming, and kicking the chair legs are all excellent ways of getting you angry. Time-out needs to be a place away from everyone else. A separate room is best. Kim used the couch for time-out. When her daughter would not sit, Kim would sit next to her and hold her down. This arrangement gave her daughter plenty of power. Her daughter was in charge of time-out, not Kim.

The Time in Time-Out

How long your child goes to time-out depends on three factors. The first factor is your child's age. For children between the ages of two and three, one or two minutes in time-out is enough. For children between the ages of three and five, two or three minutes in time-out is enough. For children five and older, use five minutes.

Be consistent about the time, even though young children do not always understand the concept of time. Use a timer. An egg timer works well. The child can see the sand falling. This helps keep them occupied. Long time-outs are no better than brief time-outs. The length of time-out does not change misbehavior. Using time-out consistently changes misbehavior.

The second factor is the seriousness of the misbehavior. Manage most misbehaviors equally. Such problem behaviors as arguing, disobedience, improper language or poor manners would all be five minute time-outs. If you feel that fighting is more serious, perhaps ten minutes would be the rule. Keep it simple. Use five minutes for most misbehaviors. Use eight or ten minutes for one or two serious misbehaviors.

The third factor is how well your child cooperates. Being uncooperative adds more time. You want time-out to work as smoothly as possible. If the standard time-out is five minutes, the time is five minutes only if your child goes to time-out willingly and sits quietly. If your child struggles on the way to time-out, double the time. Only double the time once. How to handle a child who refuses to go to time-out is discussed in the next chapter.

If your child screams or has a tantrum while in time-out, ignore it. Do not start the timer until he is quiet. Simply tell your child that he has five (or ten) minutes and that you will start the timer when he is quiet. I tell children to knock on the door when they are ready to start their time. All the time spent yelling and having a tantrum does not count. This is how some children end up spending an hour or more in time-out.

Children cry when they are unhappy. If your child whimpers a little, ignore it and let the timer continue to run. Ignore any singing, humming, story telling or poetry recitals. Do not start the timer if your child can be heard throughout the house. Treat this as an outburst. The rule is this. If your child is sobbing, singing or making noises to amuse himself, let the timer run. If he is trying to get you upset, do not start the timer. Wait for him to become quiet. Tell him to notify you when he is ready to start the time.

The Priority Misbehavior

A priority misbehavior is a specific action that you consider inappropriate or problematic. It is a priority because you want to deal with it now. It is a misbehavior that you want your child to stop doing. The priority misbehavior you select must be very specific. Examples of specific misbehaviors are fighting, arguing, talking back and swearing. Terms such as obnoxious, mean and rude are not good priority misbehaviors. These terms are not specific. They do not describe the misbehavior in a meaningful way. We all understand what these terms mean in a general sense. The problem is, these terms can be misinterpreted and create arguments. What is obnoxious to you may not be obnoxious to your child.

You may need to practice being specific. If your children misbehave a lot, it is easy to lose sight of the actual misbehaviors. "My child is always in trouble." "He never does anything the way I want him to." "She never has a good day." "He gets so obnoxious I could scream." "That child will never behave." If you find yourself thinking this way, consider exactly what it is that your child does. Carmen will not do things when asked. Francis hits his sister. Clint does not do his chores on time.

When the priority misbehavior occurs, tell your child what he has done and send him to time-out. Stay calm. Be firm and assertive.

    Mom: Greg, would you please take out the trash?

    Greg: I don't feel like it. I'll do it later.

160

> Mom: Greg, that is not obeying. Go to time-
> out. You have five minutes.

Once you tell your child that he has earned a time-out, do not change your mind. Some children will suddenly become obedient and cooperative hoping you will be lenient. Do not be fooled.

> Mom: Greg, that is not obeying. Go to time-
> out. You have five minutes.
> Greg: Okay. I'll do it now. I'll take out the
> trash.
> Mom: No. First you have to go to time-out.
> You can take out the trash when
> your time is finished.

Greg misbehaved by not taking out the trash when asked. Mom correctly enforced time-out. Greg tried tempting her by conceding to do what Mom asked. Now he has decided that taking out the trash is better than time-out. Too late. Do not surrender to these attempts. You will be encouraging your child to tease and plead and argue. Once a rule is broken, enforce time-out.

When you use time-out for the first time, begin with one misbehavior. Choose one misbehavior that you want to decrease. Do not choose the most troublesome misbehavior to start. Choose a more moderate problem. This will familiarize you and your child with time-out procedures before you attempt to tackle the big problems. Be consistent with this beginning misbehavior. Your success here sets the pattern.

When you have the first misbehavior under control, use time-out for a second misbehavior. Be cautious. You want your child to be successful. Moving ahead slowly is much safer than moving too quickly. Add new priority misbehaviors slowly and systematically to ensure feelings of success.

How to Explain Time-Out to Your Children

Sit down with each child separately and explain time-out. Timing and judgment are critical. Choose a time when things are going well. Do not try to explain time-out shortly after a blowup. Do not explain time-out when you or your child is angry. Explain that time-out is something that is going to help him behave and make better decisions. Describe time-out as time sitting alone in the bathroom (or whatever room you are going to use). Explain how the time works. Five minutes if he cooperates, longer if there is a problem. The timer will tell your child when time-out is over. If you suspect that your child may be uncooperative, explain the consequences of these actions in more detail. Finally, describe the priority misbehavior to your child. Discuss this thoroughly and give examples. Be sure he understands the misbehavior.

It is important to ignore any negative remarks that your child may make while you are explaining time-out. Don't expect enthusiasm. Simply explain time-out as specifically and as clearly as possible. Here is an example of a father and mother explaining time-out to their seven-year-old son.

Dad: Greg, could you come here please? Mom and I would like to talk with you about something.

Greg: What do you want?

Mom: You have been doing pretty well with your behavior lately in most things, but there are still times when you do not do what you are told.

Dad: We want to tell you about something

162

	that is going to help you behave and make better decisions about your behavior.
Greg:	What is it?
Mom:	It's called time-out.
Dad:	Time-out means going to the bathroom and sitting by yourself. If you go right away and you do not argue, you only have to sit for 5 minutes.
Greg:	What if I don't go?
Mom:	If you argue or don't go right away, then you will have to sit for 10 minutes.
Dad:	If you yell, or kick, or slam the bathroom door, then you will add 5 more minutes.
Greg:	Get real. I'll be in there until I'm ten.
Dad:	Do you have any questions so far?
Greg:	What a dumb idea. It will never work for me. I'm too bullheaded. Isn't that what you have been telling me?
Dad:	When you go to time-out, we will set the timer on the oven for five minutes. When you hear the buzzer, you can come out.
Mom:	But if you are noisy in there, or if you choose to have a tantrum in there, the time will not count. We will not start the timer until you are sitting quietly.
Dad:	So the sooner you sit quietly, the sooner you get out.
Mom:	Do you understand how the timer works?
Greg:	Yes. But I still don't think it will work.

Mom: If you make a mess in the bathroom, you will have to sit an extra five minutes. You will have to clean it up before you can come out. If you break anything in there, you will have to pay for it out of your allowance.

Dad: You will go to time-out when you do not do what we ask. When you do not obey us.

Mom: From now on, when we ask you to do something and you don't do it, you will go to time-out.

Dad: We hope that you won't have to go in there very often, but the choice is yours. If you obey, you won't need to go in there. It is really up to you.

Write down what you are going to say to your child. Make a list of things you want to discuss ahead of time. Here is an outline that will help you stay on track when explaining time-out to your child.

Explain these points:

Time-out is going to help improve behavior.
What time-out is.
How the time works.
The use of the timer.
Describe and give an example of the priority misbehavior.

You must remember to:

Choose a good time to talk.
Ignore any negative comments from your child.
Stay calm no matter what happens.

164

What To Say When Time-Out is Over

For most misbehaviors, start fresh when your child completes time-out. If your daughter went to time-out for swearing, change the subject when she exits. Do not lecture her on the evils of using improper language. Your words will likely land on deaf ears. The time to explain right and wrong is later, when your daughter is more receptive.

Here is an example:

>   Sarah: (Says a bad word)
>   Mom: Sarah, that's swearing. Go to time-out.
>
>   (Five minutes later, Sarah comes out of time-out.)
>
>   Mom: Have you seen my calculator anywhere?
>   (Mom changes the subject — to start fresh.)

Here is what NOT to do:

>   (Sarah comes out of time-out.)
>
>   Mom: Now aren't you sorry you said that word?
>   Sarah: No!
>   Mom: Then you march right back into time-out
>   and do not come out until you are sorry!

If your child went to time-out for refusing to do something, then he must do the task when he comes out of time-out. If your son went to time-out for refusing to set the table, he must set the table when he comes out. If he refuses, send him back to time-out. Doing time-out is not a trade for setting the table. Do not let his refusal to set the table delay dinner. That would give him power. If you suspect that your son may not cooperate, ask him to set the table an hour before dinner time. This would give him plenty of chances to set the table. Spending an entire hour in time-out (five minutes at a time) may encourage him to be more cooperative.

Here is a caution about time-out and chores. Having household jobs teaches children responsibility. Jobs give children an opportunity to accomplish something and feel proud. (See Chapter 25.) I have known some parents who expect their children to do several hours of housework every day. Children resent working if it becomes burdensome. Children need responsibilities, but they also need to be children. They should not spend hours each day doing housework. Do not use time-out to make servants of your children.

You Can't Win If You Don't Keep Score

Keep a record or chart of your child's time-out. Charting helps you be consistent. It is easy to be consistent with a new idea, just as it is easy to diet for three days. As the novelty wears off, we get lazy. Charting makes you stay consistent. The chart will show that your child goes to time-out less and less. Looking at the chart will make you and your child feel successful. Feeling successful will keep both of you motivated. You and your child would be achieving your goal. A sample chart appears at the end of this chapter.

Count the number of time-outs per day or per week. If the number of time-outs goes down, the system is working fine. Do not be discouraged if your child's chart does not show improvement quickly. Some children need more time. Some children are persistent and resist change. Some children have several good days and then a few bad days. Some children may even misbehave more at first. They want you to think that no matter what you try to do, it won't work. "I'll show you."

Charting is important because the rate of improvement varies from child to child. Some children improve dramatically in less than a week. If this happens to your child, you will believe that time-out works well. Some children are more persistent in their misbehavior. Improvement is much slower and more difficult to see on a day to day basis. It may take several weeks before you see significant improvement. You will be tempted to stop using time-out and add it to the "We have tried everything" list. Your child may average four time-outs a day the first week. At the end of two weeks, he may average three time-outs a day. This is a small improvement. A chart will show small improvements. A chart will keep you from being discouraged if large improvements do not occur right away. There will be days that you will need all the encouragement you can get.

Many days may pass with no time-outs. Then several time-outs will occur within a few days. Some children test more than others. Every once in a while, your child will test you to see if anything has changed. He needs assurance that you still mean what you say. Charting will let you know if this happens with your child.

Sometimes time-outs increase because you are having bad days. Maybe you have let your children get away with a bit more misbehavior than usual. You have not been as consistent as you need to be. Maybe your focus is negative. You have forgotten to look for good behavior.

"Go Ahead, I Like Time-Out"

What if your child says, "Go ahead. I like time-out. It gives me a chance to get away from the rest of this crazy family for a few minutes." Many clever children make statements like this. It may be true. Notably the part about getting a break from the rest of the family. Ignore these remarks completely. This will not be easy. Do not start lecturing and moralizing. Do not respond with, "There must be something wrong with you if you like time-out." This will only convince your child that your button is being pushed. Do not get trapped into believing everything your child says. If you want to evaluate time-out, do not ask your child. Look at the time-out chart.

What If There Is No Improvement?

It only means there is no improvement — yet. For most parents, the reason time-out does not work is because they are too impatient. We want quicker results for our hard work. Children learn to be more persistent than their parents. Children know that if they are stubborn long enough, Mom and Dad will give in; just like all the other times.

Keep charts on time-out for several weeks. With some children, a little improvement is all you get at first. Ask yourself these questions.

Am I being consistent? Am I following through every time the priority misbehavior occurs? You cannot skip a few times. If you only follow through when you feel like it, you will make the problem worse. You will be teaching your child that being persistent in a negative way pays off.

Am I getting angry when I use time-out? Some children want you to get angry. This is their goal. They would gladly serve several time-outs as long as they can "push your button" each time. Getting you angry may be a bigger reward than any amount of time-out. In other words, the punishment of time-out is outweighed by the reward of your anger.

Am I giving my child too much attention when I use time-out? Do not engage in long discussions and explanations. Do not let time-out pull you away from other children or other responsibilities for long talks. Five minutes in time-out is a good trade for some of mom's or dad's individual attention. If time-out seems more like a game than a punishment, you are giving too much attention.

Am I forgetting to be positive about good behavior? You cannot use time-out alone and expect it to work. Use time-out as part of a total plan. Spend more energy on the positive than the negative. If you only concentrate on misbehavior, time-out will not be as effective.

Summary

A parent recently told me that time-out changed her entire family. For years, she and her husband would yell and spank. The children would yell in return. Her seven-year-old son summed it up best. "I like time-out, Mom. It's better than what we used to do."

Time-out is a mild form of punishment that works. Use time-out with determination and planning. Arrange time-out in advance. This will teach your children how to predict the consequences of their behavior and make better decisions. Use time-out consistently. Each time the priority misbehavior occurs, use time-out. Be calm and in control of the situation when you use time-out. If you get angry, you are using time-out incorrectly.

Your Turn

Be specific when you think about priority misbehaviors. Being specific helps you focus. This exercise will help you practice being specific. Put an X in front of the statements that describe a specific misbehavior.

___1. Mark hits his sister.

___2. Sarah refuses to do the dishes.

___3. Ed is obnoxious.

___4. Joe is hyperactive.

___5. Billy is running through the house.

___6. Sue nags her brother.

___7. Mary argues when you ask her to do something.

Answers: 1, 2, 5, 6 and 7 are specific. Number 3 is not specific because of the word "obnoxious." It does not describe the misbehavior in a meaningful way. This is also true for number 4. "Hyperactive" does not tell us exactly what Joe does when he misbehaves.

Suppose you planned to use time-out for Mark, Sarah, Billy, Sue and Mary. How would you use positive feedback to strengthen an opposite, positive behavior for each of these children?

Mark: Compliment Mark when he plays nicely with his sister.

Sarah: Look for work completed. Thank her for doing her jobs.

Billy: Compliment him when he walks calmly through the house.

Sue: Catch Sue saying something pleasant to her brother.

Mary: When Mary does something without an argument, draw her attention to it. "Thanks for setting the table without an argument."

Time-Out Chart

Child's Name _____

Date	Start Time	End Time	Misbehavior	Comments

Use this chart to keep a record of your child's time-outs. Each time he receives a time-out, record the date, the time he went to time-out (Time Start) and the time he came out of time-out (Time End). Record the misbehavior and any comments. For example:

Date	Start Time	End Time	Misbehavior	Comment
6/20	12:35	12:40	Not Listening	Okay!
6/20	5:45	5:55	Not Listening	Argued - extra 5 min.
6/21	10:25	10:30	Not Listening	Went right away

Chapter 20

How To Manage A Child Who Refuses To Go To Time-Out

The way you manage a child who refuses to go to time-out depends on the age and size of your child. For children up to five or six, it is acceptable to pick them up and put them in time-out. Be careful not to hurt your child or yourself. If your child will not stay in time-out, hold the door closed from the outside. Some parents have to do this at first.

Holding a door closed is an intense physical drain. You may feel terrible. Both parents should take turns or have another adult nearby to call on for assistance. It makes more sense to hold the door closed for a few minutes than give in. While you are holding the door closed, it is essential that you remain calm. Control of yourself and the situation. Occasionally remind your child with a calm voice: "As soon as you sit quietly, I will start the timer." If you are uncomfortable with this technique, try the next idea.

With older children or younger children who are too strong to control physically, you need a different approach. When your child refuses to go to time-out, wait a minute and ask again. If you are finding yourself getting angry, walk away and cool off for a few minutes. Do not argue or yell.

Give Your Child a Minute to Think

It is all right to give your child a minute to think about what is going to happen next. "Before this goes any further, think about what it will mean. You are going to lose your bike. You will still have to serve your time-out. I am not going to argue with you. It's up to you. Why not do your time and get it over?" Sometimes, children make poor decisions. Give them a minute to think. They may realize that ten minutes in time-out is better than a long hassle.

Take Away the Treasure

If your child refuses to go to time-out after your second request, it's time to go for something treasured. Take away the privilege or activity or toy that is most loved by your child. If possible, choose something that you can lock up or put away. Things like bicycles, CD players, computers, video games, televisions, stereos and video cassette players work well. I do not know what your child's favorite plaything is, but you do. Whatever it is, that's what you lock up. The treasure goes to time-out.

If your son treasures riding his bicycle and he refuses to go to time-out, lock up his bicycle. Keep it locked until he completes his ten minutes of time-out. (Add five minutes to the original five minutes because he did not cooperate.)

Some children will push you to the limit every time hoping you will give in. They will never go to time-out until you go for the bicycle. By the time you lock up the bicycle, they have done the ten minutes. Then you have to go unlock the bicycle. You can be manipulated by this type of arrangement. If you have a loophole in your plan, your children will find it.

You can correct this situation by keeping the bicycle locked until 24 hours after your child serves the time-out. If your child starts time-out when you lock up the bicycle, return the bicycle in 24 hours and 10 minutes. If your child waits two hours to serve time-out, return the bicycle 24 hours after that. You may have to add that he is on full restriction until he regains his bicycle.

This backup strategy works well. Do everything you can (except argue and get angry) to convince your child that serving 5 or 10 minutes is better than losing his bicycle for a day. Once you start taking privileges away, the misbehavior may escalate because your child may want to get even.

If you anticipate that your child may refuse to go to time-out, then discuss the backup procedures when you first explain time-out.

Greg: What are you going to do if I won't go to time-out?

Dad: We will lock up your bicycle. You will get your bicycle back when you do your time-out.

Mom: If that doesn't convince you, then we will have to do something else, like locking up your bicycle for a whole day.

Greg: But that's not fair.

Dad: Well, Greg, as I said before, the choice is yours. We hope we never have to lock up your bicycle. We hope it never happens. But that is what we will do if we have to. That's a promise.

Whatever backup plan you come up with, be sure that your child's refusal to go to time-out costs your child an inconvenience, not you. Do not threaten backup punishments that cost you more than they cost your child. Do not say, "We cannot go out for dinner until you do your time-out." This gives your child control over you and the entire family.

Many parents are confused about taking a privilege away as a backup for time-out. Why not lock up the bicycle from the beginning and forget time-out? Time-out is something that is short and easy to administer. It is something that makes punishment easier for you in the long run. Time-out is easier than locking up the bicycle several times a week. If you take too many privileges away, your child may become discouraged and then give up trying to improve his behavior.

Summary

When a younger child refuses to go to time-out, it is acceptable to pick him up and put him in time-out. When an older child refuses to go to time-out, give him a minute to think, then take away the treasure. Be sure that your child's refusal costs him more than it costs you.

Chapter 21

How To Be Creative With Time-Out

You forgot to set the alarm. You were going to iron in the morning. Cheers for the wrinkled look. Everyone gets bread and butter. The toaster is too slow. You say a little prayer that the car cooperates today. Ever start your day this way?

Why do children pick these mornings to be irritating and oppositional? Children are opportunists. They like taking advantage of stressful situations. They like to test you when you are rushed. They like to test you when you are on the phone, at church, or at Grandmas. They like testing you when you have company.

Children know when time-out is difficult to enforce. They have a sixth sense about this. Children seem to misbehave when there is no time or place for time-out. Using time-out in these predicaments would be more of an inconvenience to you.

If your child misbehaves but you must be off to work, use delayed time-out. Tell your child that he will have to serve time-out later that afternoon. Remember to follow through. Write it down on your to-do list. Use delayed time-out for any inconvenient situation.

The same strategy applies when you ask your child to do something and later that day you notice that it was not done. He should go to time-out and then do what you asked earlier. Your child will resist. "I'll vacuum the carpet now." You may be tempted to let your child do the task and forget time-out. That would be inconsistent.

Time-Out Away From Home

Discipline begins at home. If you are positive and consistent, your child's behavior will improve. It will improve at home. It will improve everywhere. Not overnight. Gradually things will get better. Teach your children that you mean what you say. If you have not taught your children this at home, do not try to teach them at the grocery store.

Is there anything you can do at the supermarket? One alternative is to stop your shopping and return home. Send your child to time-out. Then you both return to the store and try again. Some parents have done this. It sounds crazy, but chances are you will only have to do it once. It is time consuming, however, it works well, especially with young children.

An alternative would be to use the car or car seat. Josh was three. Mom took him to the bank. It was Friday. The lines were long and slow. Josh decided to misbehave. Mom got out of line and took him to his car seat. He sat there for two minutes while mom stood behind the car watching him. He settled down and they returned to the bank. This is a good example of consistency. Mom knew it was worth it to teach Josh that misbehaving is not permitted. She was thinking about the future.

Establish a time-out setting at places you visit regularly. Use the bathroom at Grandma's. Use the laundry room at Diane's house. Another alternative is to promise time-out when you get home. Do not threaten your child with time-out. Promise time-out. Children know that threats are meaningless. A promise is a commitment. You must follow through with time-out when you get home. If you are consistent with time-out at home and in public, your child's behavior will improve.

Time-Out for Two

What should you do when two (or more) of your children misbehave at the same time? It is best to avoid discussions about who started it. This usually leads to more arguing and more disagreement. If both children have misbehaved, then both should go to time-out. Not together. One child sits while the other does time-out, and then trade places. Flip a coin to see who goes first.

Time-Out for Tiny Tots

Leah's first exposure to time-out occurred when she was about a year old. Leah toddled up to play with the TV, I picked her up and put her in the playpen. The playpen was empty and in another room. I said "No TV." I stood there for about 30 seconds and then took her out of the playpen. I said, "No TV" and put her down on the floor.

Naturally, she darted for the TV, so I repeated the same procedure. Into the playpen she went. I said "No TV." When she got out, she crawled nonstop for the TV. It took five repetitions, but she finally stopped. It wasn't the last time she tried playing with the TV. Every time she tried, she found herself in the playpen. We were very consistent about this.

We were teaching Leah not to play with the TV. We were also teaching her something more important. We were teaching the meaning of the word "No." We were laying the foundation for our parental authority.

You can use time-out with children between the ages of one and two years. Be cautious. Children at this age do not fully understand language. These children are naturally curious. They have an abundance of energy and do not like to stay in one place. Their attention span is only a few seconds long. They are easily upset and they cry a lot. They have a knack for getting into trouble. They do not realize that putting a fork in an electrical outlet is a bad idea. Children at this age do not know right from wrong. Do not think of their actions as misbehavior.

Use time-out to teach young children what is acceptable and what is not acceptable. Use time-out to teach what is safe and what is not safe. Use time-out to teach toddlers that screaming to get what they want is not appropriate. You can also use time-out to teach them not to do certain things, like playing with the television.

Some parents have asked about using a crib for time-out with infants. Cribs are supposed to be a place for comfort and sleep. Using a crib for time-out would cause the infant to associate his crib with displeasure.

For young children, use an empty playpen for time-out. Do not give away your playpen if your infant has outgrown it. Now it has another use. Many parents purchase a second playpen. One for toys — one to use for time-out. You may want to put the playpen in a spare room. When you put your child in time-out, always stand nearby. Time-out should last between 30 seconds and 1 minute. Whenever possible, tell your child what he is doing that you do not like. Keep it simple, such as "No TV" or "No plugs" or "No crayons on the wall."

Manage tantrums differently. If your child is having a tantrum because he wants a cracker, you may want to leave your child in the playpen until the screaming stops. You may need to walk away, just out of his field of view before he will stop. Peek at him every few seconds. The moment the crying stops, take your child out of the playpen. Say, "You stopped crying. Good for you." Redirect his tantrum. "It's hard for me to listen to whining. How do you ask for a cracker?" If he does not stop crying after two or three minutes, pick him up and redirect him anyway.

Summary

Be creative when you use time-out. Children know when it is difficult for you to use time-out. These situations are the test. Promise time-out at a later time. Then follow through. Do not forget. Write it on your to-do list for the day. Use time-out consistently and misbehavior will change.

Modify time-out for very young children. Do not think of time-out as a punishment for very young children. Think of time-out as a redirecting technique.

Time-Out Guidelines

Determine the time-out setting
> Safety first
> As boring as possible

Identify one priority misbehavior

Use a timer

Explain time-out to your child
> Time-out is going to improve behavior
> What time-out is
> How the time works
> How the timer works
> Describe the priority misbehavior (give an example)

Use time-out as part of a plan

Be consistent with time-out

Stay calm when you use time-out

Use a chart to keep a record of progress

Initial episodes may be difficult (extinction burst)

The time in time-out
> 5 minutes if you cooperate
> 10 minutes if you do not

Start the time when your child is sitting quietly (a little crying is okay)

The child who refuses to go
> Put little ones in
> Take away the treasure
>> until the time-out is done
>> until the time-out is done plus 24 hours
>> (or a reasonable added time)

When your child completes time-out

      Start fresh - redirect
      (if the misbehavior is over)
          or

      Your child still has to do what is asked
      (if he went to time-out for refusing a request)

Use delayed time-out
      For inconvenient times
      When away from home

Time-out for two - - flip a coin and take turns.

Chapter 22

How To Manage Arguments And Power Struggles

"Can I spend the night at Corey's house?"

"Not tonight, I'd like you to stay home with us."

"I haven't gone to Corey's in over a month."

"Not tonight, please."

"There's nothing to do here. It's boring."

"Please don't argue."

"I don't get it. Why can't I go. Give me one good reason."

"Because I said so. If you don't stop arguing, you are going to be grounded."

"Big deal. Go ahead and ground me. What's the difference. I can't ever do anything anyway."

"Okay. You're grounded for the entire weekend. Go to your room."

"I can't wait until I grow up and get out of this house."

Children love to argue. They want their ideas to be everyone else's ideas. They like to prove that they are right and you and everyone else are wrong. Children like to control the situation. They enjoy having power over their parents.

Children have a need for power. Their need for power is normal. Children see adults as having power. We do what we want to do. At least that's what our children think. We appear self-reliant and secure. We are all grown up. We have power. Children want to be like us. They want power too.

Having a need for power is not a bad thing. It is only when a child uses power in a negative way that power can become a problem. Power-seeking children try to do what they want to do. They refuse to do what you ask. Children who seek power do not like to be told what to do. They resist authority. They like to make the rules. They like to determine how things are going to be done.

Why You Can't Win a Power Struggle

Most parents deal with power by emphasizing counter control. This does not work. Efforts to control a power-seeking child often lead to a deadlock or power struggle between your child and you. No final victory is ever possible for you. Once you find yourself in a power struggle, you have lost.

If your child wins the power struggle, he is reassured that power caused the victory. You were defeated by his power. If you win the power struggle, your child thinks that it was your power that caused the victory. It was your power that defeated him. He is reassured of the value of power. This results in children striking back, again and again, each time with stronger methods. You win the battle but lose the war.

Every child displays power differently. Most power struggles are active. Arguing is a good example of active power. Some children have learned the value of passive resistance. Rather than argue, these children will refuse to do what you asked. They nod their heads and just sit quietly. Some even smile a little. This type of power has a definite purpose, to "push your button."

How to Handle Power

Stop being part of the power struggle. It takes two to have a power struggle. It takes two to argue. Make a firm commitment to yourself that you will no longer engage in arguments and lengthy explanations. State your expectations clearly and firmly and walk away. Tell your child exactly what you want him to do, when he must do it and what happens if he does not. Then walk away.

> "It's time to turn off the TV."
> "I want to watch the next show."
> "Sorry, it's time to get ready for bed."
> "Can't I stay up for one more show?"
> "Not tonight. We have to get up early."
> "We always have to get up early."
> "Turn off the TV. Get your shower and go to bed. Do it now or you will lose TV for tomorrow night."

Do not stay in the situation and argue. Go to your room and close the door if necessary. Do not let your child push your button. If you get angry, you will be rewarding your child. Your anger will give your child the power over you that he seeks. You may need to use punishment when dealing with power. Tell your child what to do. Be ready with a punishment if your child fails to cooperate. If you punish a child because of a power struggle, remember two things. Do not punish in anger. This will only encourage your child to strike back with power. Smaller punishments work better than bigger punishments. If your child thinks you have punished him too harshly, he will retaliate with power.

When your child does what you ask without an argument, thank him. Call attention to it. "Thank you. You did what I asked without an argument. I appreciate that. It shows you are cooperating." As a long term solution, remember that a child's need for power can be a positive thing. Look for independence, self-reliance, leadership and decision-making. When your child shows these qualities, spotlight them. Catch him being good. As with most behavior problems, the positive approach is the best remedy for handling power.

The Difference Between Power and Authority

The difference between power and authority lies within you. When you have to confront your children, emphasize cooperation, not control. Stay calm and rational in spite of the situation. Guard your anger button. Stop and think. Do not react impulsively. Give clear and specific expectations. Explain what will happen if your child chooses not to cooperate. Do not give ultimatums. Focus on influencing your child's motivation.

Here is an example of a parent using power.

> "Why can't I go?"
> "Because I said so. I'm your father."
> "What has that got to do with it?"
> "Everything."
> "Well I'm going anyway."
> (Dad gets angry) "I'm warning you. If you go to that party, you are going to be in big trouble."
> "Oh sure. What are you going to do?"
> "You just wait and see."

Here is an example of a parent using authority.
> "Why can't I go?"
> "I don't think it is going to be safe."
> "I can handle it."

186

"There is going to be a lot of drinking at that
party. Probably drugs too. I don't want you
there."

"I'll be okay. You don't have to worry."

"You don't understand. I trust you. That's not
the problem. I don't trust some of those other
kids. You can't control what they will do."

"Everyone else is going."

"I know you want to go very much. I know
you'll be disappointed."

"I want to go."

"Sorry. You can't go. You can do something
else. Have some kids over here."

How to Correct Your Child Without an Argument

Giving verbal corrections is difficult. Verbal correc-
tion can turn into arguments, especially if you get angry. Yelling, scolding and threatening help you vent your anger. They
do not correct misbehavior. Sometimes they make the misbehavior worse.

Stay calm. Tell your children to stop. Be ready to
enforce a punishment if you must. Do not become caught in
the cycle of yelling and threatening. You do not want to spend
the rest of your life that way. Getting angry and yelling makes
arguments worse. If your child's goal is to push your button
and get you angry, yelling is a reward for misbehaving. Yelling
will strengthen unwanted behavior.

How can you correct your children and avoid arguments? Verbal corrections are part of good discipline. The
purpose of verbal corrections is to teach better decision making. Here are some suggestions.

1. Begin by validating your relationship. "You are my son and
I love you. Nothing you do will ever change that."

2. State your concern. "Your behavior at the store was not acceptable. I was embarrassed."

3. Remind your child of previous good behavior. "That's not like you. You are always very well behaved when we go shopping."

4. Separate your child from his behavior. Say, "That behavior is unacceptable." Do not say, "Anyone who would do that is stupid."

5. React appropriately to the size of the problem. If your child misbehaves while shopping, restrict him from shopping. "You can't go shopping with me for two weeks. You will have to stay home. I hope that when you can come with me again, you will behave."

Do not ask why. Children misbehave because they choose to misbehave. When you ask why, you are suggesting there may be an excuse. "Why did you do that?" "He told me to do it." Clever children will search for excuses until they come up with one that you accept. If you don't accept it, you then have a power struggle on your hands.

Realize that an upset child is not a good listener. This is not the time for constructive communication. Wait until he cools off.

Teach your children to learn from their mistakes rather than suffer from them. Point out things they do wrong by showing them ways to do it better. "You remembered to take out the garbage. Good going. The twist ties need to be a little tighter next time. I'll show you how."

Admit you are wrong once in a while. This is a tough one. "Sorry, I was wrong. I made a mistake." Your children will learn from your example. When you openly admit your mistakes and weaknesses, you are showing them that grown-ups are not perfect. We don't know everything. Anthony attended a meeting I had with a proofreader of this book. He could not believe that she had so many suggestions. It was good for him to see that his Dad is not perfect. It was also good for him to see that I did not take the corrections personally. I explained that she was helping me make the book better. I showed him that it's okay to make errors.

Do not carry on about small mistakes. Deal with it and then let it go. The purpose of verbal corrections is to have a more cooperative youngster. Misbehaviors and mistakes are normal. You can help your child best by minimizing problems. Do not dwell on them. Do not rehash the day's problems with your spouse in front of your child. Children cannot build on weaknesses. They can only build on strengths.

These same ideas apply when your children are arguing with each other. Stay calm and do not make threats. If you can, help your children reach a settlement. Brandon and Marie have been arguing for ten minutes. Dad has had enough. Finally, he gets angry. He yells, "Stop or you will both go to bed."

Most children will quiet down for a while when threatened. Unfortunately, Dad thinks that yelling works. This is a mistake. Yelling works temporarily. The quiet will not last. Yelling and threatening have no long term effect on misbehavior. The children argue. Dad yells. They quiet down for a while. Soon, they argue again. Dad yells. They quiet down, again. This can go on and on. These children will learn that they can argue until Dad yells at them to stop. They will not learn to solve their problems.

A little humor may help. Here is a way to neutralize arguments in the car. Whenever you are on a trip and the children start to argue, ask them to stop. If they don't stop, begin talking about a trip for parents only. "This explains why so many parents leave their children at home. Next trip, let's go somewhere romantic." When children hear this, they get the point.

When Children Get Even

When a child feels hurt or angry, he may want to get even. He wants to hurt you. Getting even takes away some of his hurt and anger. Getting even makes children feel that justice has been served. Revenge is important to children because of their keen sense of fairness.

Revenge can destroy relationships between parents and children. This is especially true of teenagers. Some children embarrass you in front of others. Some children strike out at something that is special to you. Some children hurt a younger brother or sister. Some children run away. Some children will break a window or break something of value. I once worked with a mother who had a vengeful teenage son. One day she came home to find that he had thrown all of her fine china and crystal glasses into the street. Revenge is not pleasant.

Revenge typically begins when you punish your child for something he believes is unfair. He decides to get even with you by misbehaving again. He pushes your button. You get angry and punish again. He strikes back again. The cycle of retaliation begins.

Breaking the Cycle of Retaliation

The target of your child's revenge is your feelings. A child who wants to get even wants to hurt you. If he does, he has achieved his pay-off. Some parents lack self-confidence about their skills as a parent. Clever children realize this and take full advantage of the parent's weakness.

Revenge seeking children know exactly where to strike. They say things such as, "I hate you. You're a terrible mother." The reason for these remarks is to make you feel hurt. You feel that you have failed your children. They want you to feel inadequate and guilty.

When you feel inadequate or guilty, you begin to question your own judgments. *Then you begin to give in.* There is nothing a revenge seeking child would like more than for you to become inconsistent. This is the pay-off they seek.

Believe in your own abilities and you will not become the victim of your child's revenge. Support yourself. When your child strikes at your button, remain strong. Tell yourself that you are a good parent. I am doing the best I can.

Be positive when disciplining your children. Do not criticize. Be sure that punishments are fair and that they make sense to your child. Punishments should not humiliate or embarrass your child. Punishment should be mild. They should teach your child to make better decisions. Do not use punishment to get even with your child for something he has done that hurts you or makes you angry.

Control yourself. Do not let him push your button. Have faith in your judgment. Do not give in to: "Taylor's mom lets him watch R-rated movies." Do not reward your child's revenge. The more confidence that you have, the easier it will be for you to win your child's cooperation.

Many parents measure their worthiness by their children's success. "If I am a good parent, why are my kids so bad?" They feel that if their children are not perfect, then they must be less than adequate as a parent. By believing this idea, you are making yourself vulnerable to your children. You become an easy target for any child looking for a button to push.

Think about the reasons you might feel this way. Are you insecure about yourself? Do you feel this way because of your spouse? Is this a leftover belief from your relationship with your parents? Think about your strengths rather than your insecurities. The more that you focus on your strengths, the more confident you will become. Stay calm when your child says, "I hate you." Say, "I'm sorry you feel that way, but I have to do what's right."

Summary

Children like to engage parents in arguments and power struggles. They hope you will get angry. When you do, they win. Stay calm, particularly when you use punishment.

Being a good parent does not always mean that you will be your child's best friend. There have been times when my children have been angry at me. I do not like how it feels. Yet, I am not going to give in to their demands. I am not going to criticize myself. Ten years from now they will not remember the time I would not let them watch an R-rated movie. But they will remember my commitment to them. I am going to support myself because I know that what I am doing is best.

Your Turn

Robert is an active ten-year-old. He is not a malicious child, but he is usually in one kind of trouble or another. His parents love him very much, but they are fed up with his misbehavior. They try to be positive. Sometimes they forget. Dad does the punishing. He says he has tried "everything." He even tried time-out on a few occasions. When asked about Robert, Dad replies, he is always in trouble. "He gets so obnoxious I could scream. I've tried it all. We just go around in circles and argue. You should see how he treats his mother. The only thing that stops him is the paddle. I spend half my life hitting that kid. You think he would learn. It seems like every time I think about it, he is doing something to upset me. I won't give up. I'll make him behave or else." What could these parents be doing differently? Make a list of your ideas and suggestions.

Here are some ideas.

1. Robert's parents need to change their behavior first. They are trapped by Robert's misbehavior. That's all they see. He is "always" in trouble. He gets so "obnoxious." They need to be more specific. They need to look for opposite, positive behaviors, such as doing what he is asked without an argument.

2. "Dad does the punishing." Mom and Dad need to work together or Robert will manipulate and continue to mistreat Mom.

3. They have tried "everything." Robert is a persistent child. He has learned that he can out last anything his parents try. Mom and Dad need to be more patient. They need to stick with one strategy. You cannot use time-out on a few occasions. You must use it consistently.

4. Mom and Dad need to stop arguing with Robert. Dad should give up the "behave or else" attitude. This attitude creates more resistance in Robert. They need to tell Robert what he must do, when he must do it, what happens if he does, and what happens if he does not. Then they must calmly follow through.

5. Dad believes that spanking stops Robert. It does not. Robert does not behave to avoid the spanking. Spankings have not changed Robert's behavior. Try a punishment that does not provoke Robert to the point of retaliation.

Here is a chart that summarizes the difference between power and authority.

Power	Authority
Emphasize cooperation	Not Control
Stay rational	Not emotional
Keep your self-control	Do not get angry
Stop and think	Do not act impulsively
Be proactive	Not reactive
Relate consequences to behavior and choices	Do not give ultimatums
Remain child centered	Not self-centered

Chapter 23

Reducing Attention Seeking

"Mommy, come here and see my picture."
"It's very nice, Sarah."
"I can't find the blue crayon."
"It's right here."
"I can't find the green one."
"Here it is."
"I don't want to color. I want to paint."
"I'll get your paint set."
"Will you paint this flower for me, Mommy?"

Children need attention and approval. That's normal. However, this need can become a problem. Attention seeking becomes a problem when it happens all the time. Even charming attention seeking can become controlling. Many children make tragedies out of trivial concerns to get your sympathy. Excessive attention seeking results in a situation where your child commands your life.

Many children misbehave to get attention. This is the most notorious reason for misbehavior in young children. It can be the seed for discipline problems in later childhood and adolescence.

Your goal is not to eliminate your child's need for attention and approval. When handled correctly, your child's need for attention can be a helpful tool for improving your child's behavior. Do not eliminate the need for attention. Eliminate those attention seeking behaviors that are excessive or unacceptable. "Sarah, I know that you want me to stay and paint with you. I am busy now. If you can be patient and paint by yourself for ten minutes, I'll be able to spend some time with you then." Mother is giving Sarah an opportunity to have the attention that she wants and needs. Mother is not giving in to nagging.

How Much Attention is Too Much?

That depends on you. How much attention seeking can you tolerate? The rule is that children will seek as much attention as you give them. You must strike a balance between how much your children want and how much you can give. Even normal attention seeking can drive you crazy on some days.

Do not let your children's need for attention turn into demands for attention. When children do not get enough attention, they resort to outbursts, tantrums, nagging, teasing and other annoying behaviors. If I can't get attention by being good, then I'll misbehave to get Mom's attention.

Three Kinds of Attention

Adult attention and approval are among the strongest rewards for children. Unfortunately, parents seldom use attention wisely. There are three kinds of attention.

Positive Attention

Negative Attention

No Attention

When you give your children attention and approval for being well-behaved, they are getting positive attention. Positive attention means catching children being good. Focus on positive behavior. Positive attention can be words of praise or encouragement, closeness, hugs, or a pat on the back. A pleasant note in your child's lunch box works well. Positive attention increases good behavior.

When you give your child attention for misbehavior, you are giving negative attention. Negative attention typically begins when you become upset. You follow with threats, interrogation, and lectures. Negative attention is not a punishment. Negative attention is a reward. Negative attention does not punish misbehavior. Negative attention increases misbehavior.

What is the easiest way to capture your attention? Sitting quietly or misbehaving? When children do not receive attention in a positive way, they will get your attention any way they can. Do not pay attention to misbehaviors. Pay attention to good behavior.

> Jeremy and Dominic are sitting quietly and watching Saturday morning cartoons for thirty minutes. Everything is peaceful. Dad is working on the computer. Suddenly, an argument erupts. "It's my turn to pick a show." Dad charges into the room. He turns off the television, scolds the two children, and sends them to their rooms.

For thirty minutes, these children were well behaved. Dad said nothing to them about how well they were doing. Nothing was said about how quiet they were. Nothing was said about how well they were cooperating. The moment there was trouble, Dad was instantly mobilized. Dad did not give them any positive attention while they were being good. When they began misbehaving, Dad rushed in with plenty of negative attention.

Negative attention teaches children how to manipulate and get their way. They learn to be troublesome. They learn how to interrupt you. They learn how to control you. Negative attention teaches children how to tease, nag and annoy. It teaches children to aggravate, irritate and exasperate. We teach this by not paying attention to our children when they are behaving appropriately. We teach this by paying attention to them when they are misbehaving.

198

I have worked with hundreds of parents who have taught their children to be negative attention seekers. I have never met a parent who taught this deliberately. When you attend to the negative and ignore the positive, you teach your children to behave in a negative way. You teach your children to misbehave to get attention. Your child will misbehave to get your attention in the future.

Do not wait for misbehavior to happen. Do not take good behavior for granted. We do this with teenagers. We come to expect good behavior. We overlook their efforts. When a child demonstrates good behavior, notice it. Look for it. The more you notice, the more you will find. You will get more good behavior in the future. Anyone can catch children being bad. Turn this around. Catch them being good. It's not easy. It takes practice.

Statistics show that the average American parent spends seven minutes a week with each of their children. Do better than average. Telling your children that you love them is not enough. Show them that you love them. Spend ten minutes of quality time with each child every day. No excuses, like I was just too busy today or I didn't have time. We are all too busy.

In many families, both parents work. Some parents work two jobs. Your most important job is being a parent. When you come home after work, give the first thirty minutes to your children. Do not be the parents whose only hour with their daughter this week was in the principal's office or at the police station. Write your children into your plan book. Make an appointment with each of your children every day. Go for a walk and listen to what is happening in their lives. Turn off the TV for an hour and talk.

How to Ignore

When you ignore misbehaviors you are giving no attention. Because attention is rewarding to children, withholding attention can be an effective punishment. Withholding attention can weaken a misbehavior. When your child misbehaves to get your attention, ignore the misbehavior. Ignore your child's inappropriate demands for attention. You will weaken those demands. You will extinguish the misbehavior.

Some parents find this hard to believe. Some parents think that if a child is misbehaving he must be punished. This belief is not true. Ignoring demands for attention is the best cure. When you ignore consistently, you will teach your child that these misbehaviors are not paid off with attention. Temper tantrums need an audience. Take the audience away and there is no point of having a tantrum. *Do not forget to redirect.* Teach children appropriate ways to get attention. "My ears do not listen to whining. Please ask in a soft voice."

When to Ignore

Ignoring does not mean to ignore the problem. It means to ignore demands for negative attention. There are many misbehaviors that you should not ignore. Some misbehaviors should be punished. Deciding when to ignore or when to punish is not easy. There are no exact rules. It takes timing and judgment. When your child misbehaves to get attention, ignore it. If your child does not stop in two or three minutes, give him a reminder. Tell your child, "I do not respond to whining. When you stop, we'll talk." Wait another minute or two. If he still does not stop, then tell your child to stop or he will be punished. "Stop now or you will go to time-out."

If you get angry or let your child push your button, you lose. If you must use a punishment, dispense the punishment without anger. If you get angry, then your child has succeeded in getting the negative attention that he was after. If you feel yourself getting angry, walk away. Cool off. If you give in, you will be providing your child with an attention payoff. You will be rewarding a misbehavior.

Summary

Give your children positive attention when they are behaving. Do not take good behavior for granted. Ignore demands for attention such as teasing and whining. Giving attention to these demands encourages children to misbehave to get attention. Understanding these ideas is easy. Practicing them is difficult. You are worth it. Make the commitment. Your children are worth it too.

Part V: SIMPLE SOLUTIONS TO PREVAILING PROBLEMS

Chapter 24

Resolving Conflicts Between Siblings

Parents often ask about sibling rivalry. Most problems between siblings do not involve rivalry. They involve conflict. Conflicts between children have occurred since Adam and Eve decided that Cane needed a little brother.

Children experience conflicts for many of the same reasons that adults do. Children want the circumstances in their lives to be on their own terms. They want the rules to fit their behavior rather than fit their behavior to the rules. Children can only see their side of a situation. Children want everything to go their way. When they do not get what they want, they become angry.

It should not be surprising that anytime you put two or three people who think this way into the same confined space and tell them to play and have fun, you are likely to get some conflict. So what can parents do to reduce the amount of conflict among their children? Begin by using a conflict as an opportunity to learn. Teach your children acceptable ways of expressing disappointment and resentment. Teach them how to manage their feelings without violating the other person.

> "You know Alyssa, it's okay to be angry at your brother for teasing you. But it is not okay to hit him. What else could you have done? Let's think about other things to do when you get angry."

This approach will not work if your child is still upset about the altercation. Communication is always more effective when everyone has had time to cool off. It also helps to intervene early, before tempers erupt.

> "It sounds to me like you two may be getting into an argument. I believe that you can work this out for yourselves and I hope you do. If you need my help, let me know. But if you can't solve this on your own, you will need to take a little break from each other for a while."

This type of message empowers your children to believe they can resolve their conflict. If you believe they can, they are likely to believe the same. Yet it also sets a limit. Knowing when to become involved and when to keep out takes judgment. As a rule, always encourage your children to solve their own conflicts. Give them time to do this. Then if you see that their conflict is escalating rather than resolving, you may need to guide them to think of a solution. Simply separate them for a few minutes, to give them time to think.

Teach your children to respect the other person even when you do not agree. This is a skill that will be helpful when they become adults. "You do not have to agree with what your brother says. He sees it his way and you see it your way. It is okay to have different opinions about this, but it's not okay to fight." In some situations, it can also help if you add something about seeing the conflict from the other person's point of view. "Each of you has a reason for thinking that your opinion is correct." Then have the children exchange their reasons and develop a compromise. Each child has to give a little so that both can be satisfied.

As a long-term prevention, focus on the positive social behaviors in your children. Compliment your children for getting along. Parents forget this. It is easy to take good behavior for granted. This is a mistake. Look for cooperation and sharing. Then reinforce it. "I appreciate you playing together so well. Thank you. I hope you both feel proud of yourselves."

Summary

Perhaps the most important thing a parent can do to teach their children better methods of conflict resolution is to be a good example. Model appropriate ways of solving the conflicts you encounter in your life — with your spouse, your boss, your neighbor, even the irritating sales clerk. Do not store anger; express it constructively. "When you continue to argue, I get angry because it's so frustrating to go around in circles." Show your children that there are prudent ways to disagree. Model calmness, politeness and respect for the other person. Remember to be patient. If your children have developed patterns of arguing and fighting, it will take time to change. Hang in there. They are worth it.

Chapter 25

Responsibility, Chores and Allowance

Children need to learn the value of work. When children learn to do work around the house, they are actually learning the basics of independent living skills. Responsibility builds confidence and self-esteem. Work teaches cooperation and teamwork.

Do not give your children too many jobs or responsibilities. This can cause resentment. Accept your child's best effort even though the finished product may not be up to your standard. A good attitude is more important than a perfectly made bed. Being a helper is more important than having all the spoons in the correct drawer divider. Teaching children to work takes more time than doing the work yourself. Use plenty of positive feedback for effort and for jobs well done.

Model appropriate attitudes about work. Children need to see that housework and chores are a part of life. Illustrate the satisfaction you feel when you complete a tough job. Work side-by-side with your children and have fun. Whistle while you work, so to speak! Let your children have some say in their chores. Giving children choices reduces resistance. Assign small responsibilities to young children and then increase the difficulty as they grow older. Responsibilities grow with your child. There are some examples at the end of this chapter.

Model responsibility. Complaining about housework only teaches children to complain. Parents often talk to me about their children's lack of responsibility, yet they are late for appointments. Be prompt. Use "to do" lists, checklists, planners. Teach children these techniques.

As children grow older, they want more privileges. Link responsibilities with privileges. The more you do the more you earn. Parents expect more from children as they grow. In turn, offer more freedom and more choices. Negotiate responsibilities. "You think about what is fair and then we will discuss it." Some parents have found it helpful to increase privileges and responsibilities with each birthday — a kind of annual promotion.

Talk about goals. Begin early so your children will be familiar with setting goals before they are teenagers. Early goals are experiences such as learning to ride a bicycle, swimming, or skating. Goals expand with maturity. What grades do they expect for themselves? What can I achieve athletically? What are reasonable careers? What are the advantages of going to college?

Working for Earnings

Many parents take allowance money away from a child who does not complete all his chores. Make this strategy positive. Use charts as a means to earn allowance. This works well with any child. It works remarkably well with teenagers. Make a list of jobs to do around the house. Call the list "Money-makers." Each job is worth an amount of money. The child who does the job gets the money as part of an allowance. Distribute jobs fairly among your children. Do not give your child a set allowance and then take money away. Start each week with no money and let him earn as he works. Children are more able than we think. There are many household jobs children can do. Working teaches children that everyone can pitch in and help.

Money Making Chart

	Mon	Tue	Wed	Thur	Fri
Rachel	Garbage 7:00-7:10 10 pts.		Set Table 4:30-4:45 15 pts.		Bathroom 4:00-4:30 30 pts.
Andy		Set Table 4:30-4:45 15 pts.		Garbage 7:00-7:10 10 pts.	Furniture 4:00-4:30 30 pts.
Jan	Laundry 4:00-4:15 10 pts.			Set Table 4:30-4:45 15 pts.	Vacuum 4:00-4:30 30 pts.

You can use one chart for all your children's jobs. Assign a start time, completion time, and a point value to each job. Distribute the jobs so that older children work more and earn more. This teaches children that responsibilities and privileges come with age. Rotate jobs when necessary. Each point could be worth five cents in allowance.

This arrangement teaches children to remember when it is time to do a job. If a child fails to start by the appointed time, another child may then do the job and get the points. If Andy has not started to set the table by 4:30, Janelle may set the table. She would then get Andy's 15 points. Andy may want to argue that the job is his. Simply say the job was his until 4:30. At that time it became the job of anyone willing to work.

If the job is not finished by the appointed completion time, your child does not earn the points. Let him finish the job if he chooses, but no points. If he refuses to finish the job, allow another child to finish. Award this child the points.

Be firm but fair. If your child works diligently during the allotted time but does not finish, you have not assigned enough time. In this case, be reasonable. Let the child finish and award him the points. Then change the time on the chart. Start sooner or allow more time to finish. Make this change only if the time turns out to be unfair. Do not change if your child is being stubborn or lazy.

A parent told me that this technique changed her life. Her children stopped arguing about chores. They realized that if they did not work as asked, a brother or sister was going to get their allowance. If you only have one child, ask a neighbor child to do the job and then pay him your child's allowance. You will not have to do this very often.

Teaching Children the Value of Money

Explain the use of money. Begin as early as age three. Explain why and how you buy items at the store. Money is necessary. Money comes from working. It does not appear by magic from the ATM machine. My son learned the use of money at age three. He learned that he could play a game of PacMan with one of those "little round silver things."

Do not pay for everything. You should not pay your child for everything he does. It is better to assign some jobs as responsibilities without pay. This teaches the idea that we all need to contribute to the success of the family. After your child completes required duties, allow him to pick from a Money-maker list. Some things you do as part of the family. Some things can earn money. You can also have bonus jobs for earning extra money. When your child or teenager needs a few extra dollars for a special activity or event, let them earn the money by doing a special job, such as cleaning the yard or waxing the car.

Introduce expenses. As children mature and allowances increase, require them to use their own money for some things. This applies to dating, movies, CD's, and other entertainment. Children who want designer labels should pay the additional cost. When Anthony was in fifth grade, he wanted a pair of labeled tennis shoes that retailed for $125.00. I offered to pay the first $40.00. This is what I would pay for good tennis shoes without the label. The rest of the money was up to him. He went to work in the neighborhood doing odd jobs. In about a month, he had enough money. He was proud of himself. He wore them every day. He took such nice care of these shoes that when he outgrew them a year later, they still looked new. He took such nice care of them because he had considerable ownership in them.

Teach consumerism. Have children compare prices. What size package gives the best value? Explain why you choose certain products. Teach about inflation by going to the library and reading ads in old newspapers. This is fun. Remember when a loaf of bread was a quarter? You should know that Anthony did not pay $125 for his shoes. He called all over town until he found them on sale — $90. He was a wise consumer, especially with his own money.

Teach home budgeting. Explain how a finite amount of money needs to be distributed for housing, food, clothing, utilities, car expenses, etc. Do not shelter children from this. Include older children in family financial planning. Have them write out the checks for the monthly bills.

Start a savings account. Most children comprehend the meaning of savings by age ten. Children are impulsive spenders. Encourage your children to save a certain percentage of their income. Some parents match savings.

Start a checking account. Most 16-year-olds are ready for a limited checking account and limited credit card. Teach them to manage these tools while you are still around to keep things from getting out of control.

Set financial goals. Discuss plans for paying for college. Research college scholarships and aid programs. Have them calculate tuition cost and living expenses.

Earn their own money. The best way for children to learn about money is for them to get their own job when they are legally old enough. Help them find a job that is safe, has reasonable hours and includes friendly people. Having your own income is a great self-esteem booster.

Do not over do it! Children need to learn about the value of money. They need to learn how to earn and manage money. But do not worship money. Spending money on something impractical occasionally is fun and human.

Summary

If parents used encouragement as often as they use criticism, children would behave more responsibly. Do not make all your children's decisions for them. They need to learn for themselves. Some children need to fail a little before they appreciate success.

Adolescence is a time of great personal insecurity. Stay involved with your teenagers without being intrusive. Do not assume that responsibility appears suddenly at age sixteen. Adolescents still need help taking care of themselves. Teenagers need just as much love, support, encouragement and time as younger children.

Chores and Allowances

Many parents give children a weekly allowance then take money away for not completing work. Reverse this - use a positive strategy.

Start each week with no money and build.
(work = allowance).

Specific jobs earn a certain amount of money.

Be sure jobs are age appropriate.

Do not pay children for everything they do around the house.

Some jobs are required, some are for allowance.

Required jobs must be done first.

Have bonus jobs available for extra money when needed.

How to Teach Your Children About Responsibility

Sit down with each of your children and divide activities and responsibilities into three categories. Some things are required behaviors; some things are negotiated; some things are totally up to your child. Make a list of each category. As your child grows and shows responsibility, move more items toward the bottom list. For example, wearing make-up may start on the negotiated list. Give your daughter some choice about her use of make-up but you still have to approve. As she matures and shows good taste in her use of make-up, you could move this activity to the bottom list. "You have shown that you use make-up correctly. From now on, you won't need to check with me. I trust you to take care of this yourself." This strategy will help your child see the value in responsible behavior.

REQUIREMENTS —What your child has to do.
  Earn passing grades
  Help with work around the house

NEGOTIATED — Your child has some choice but needs
  your approval.
  Curfew
  TV programs
  Make-up
  Snacks

SELF CONTROL — Your child has total responsibility.
  Sports
  Music
  School activities

Age Appropriate Responsibilities

3 to 4-year-olds
Brushing teeth
Put dirty clothes in the laundry
Match socks
Put clean clothes away with assistance
Help pick up room and toys

4 to 5-year-olds
Help set or clear table of unbreakables
Water plants
Feeding pets
Get the mail or newspaper with parent watching
Wash and dry plastic dishes
Help load dishwasher with safe items

6 to 8-year-olds
Clean own room
Take care of most personal hygiene
Help fold and sort laundry
Make beds
Put away groceries
Set and clear table
Wash and dry dishes (not sharp objects)
Take out garbage
Sweep floors

9 to 12-years-olds
All personal hygiene
Polish furniture
Prepare parts of meals
Do some laundry
Help with yard work
Help cleaning pool

Vacuum carpet
Mop floors
Prepare own snacks
Help with grocery shopping
Purchase clothing with assistance
Clean the garage
Washing the car

13 to 15-year-olds
Baby-sitting
Mowing lawns
Clean windows
Help with heavy cleaning
Do own laundry
Do some ironing
Budget own money
Shop for own clothing
Do neighborhood jobs
Do small repairs
Prepare some meals

16 years plus
Do outside jobs for money
Plan and prepare meals
Travel with supervision
Take care of all clothing needs
Help care for the automobiles
Plan higher education goals

Chapter 26

Homework Hassles

Homework is one of the greatest sources of conflict between children and parents. Children avoid doing homework. They procrastinate until the last minute. They fail to bring it home. They make excuses. They do as little as possible. They take too long. They do it too fast. They do not do their best. Parents become frustrated and angry with these attitudes and behaviors. The source of this frustration is often disappointment. We want perfect apples. Parents become embarrassed when children perform poorly on their homework. What will the teacher think of me?

Most parents realize the value of homework. Most children do not. Parents know that homework reinforces skills. Practice makes perfect. Children see homework as repetitive and busywork. Parents know that children who do quality homework learn more and get better grades. Some children see homework as a penalty for not getting everything done at school.

Parents and teachers need to be partners in the development of healthy homework habits in children. Teachers need to explain the value of homework to their students. Teachers need to explain that homework is to help you learn. It impacts your grades and your future. Homework develops responsibility, independence and accountability. It develops personal organization skills and teaches children to manage their time.

Teachers have a responsibility to ensure that homework is not busywork. Teachers also need to ensure that the homework is well within the child's ability level. The assignment must be fair. If your child works for a solid hour to do an assignment that looks as if it should take ten minutes, call the teacher immediately. The homework needs to be modified. The assumption is that your child is working diligently, not dawdling.

Teachers should also have an incentive program that motivates children to complete homework on time and with their best effort. Some teachers use class charts. Students who successfully complete homework earn stars that are traded for class activity time. Most primary teachers agree with using an incentive program. Some upper grade, junior high and high school teachers often do not agree with using incentives to motivate children to do homework. These teachers believe that children should do homework because it is a demonstration of responsibility. This is true. Children need to learn the value of studying. However, if a child does not have the internal motivation to complete homework, charts and contracts often provide some external motivation to get things going in the right direction. If your child is not motivated and the teacher does not have an incentive program, you can develop a program at home.

How to be a Homework Facilitator

There are several factors to consider when developing successful homework strategies. Visit or call your child's teacher and ask about his or her homework policy. How often will homework be given? How much homework will there be? What subjects? Ask to be notified in advance when special projects are due. When are the tests? Will there be study guides? This information will enable you to develop a better homework plan.

Children need to know that doing homework is their job not yours. Many parents have to stand over their children each night. Every assignment is a struggle. Homework is between your child and his teacher. You are only a facilitator. Your job is to help -- not do it for him. Do not make this mistake. If you are already trapped in this dilemma, stop tonight. Tell your child that your responsibility is to help. His responsibility is to complete the homework. Here is what you can do to help.

Be sure your child has enough time to do homework. Children are involved in many activities: athletics, music lessons, dance class, scouts, church clubs. These are excellent, but homework must be the priority. Have a set time for homework each day. Negotiate this time with your children if possible. Reschedule around other activities only when necessary. Check with your child's teacher to determine how much time will be needed. If your child has no homework, he can read from his favorite book for 30 minutes. The same is true for a child who "forgets" his homework. These techniques let children know that homework is important.

Have a specific place to do homework. This place should be distraction free. Turn off the TV during homework time. Parents can set an example by reading. Be sure your child has a table and chair. The kitchen table works fine, as long as there is quiet. Be sure there is adequate lighting. Have all necessary supplies nearby so that homework time is not spent hunting for glue or tape or paper. Your child's teacher can give you a list of items to put into a supply box. Older children may need a calculator and eventually a computer.

Some children resist doing homework. The first thing to do is to be sure the child can do the homework. Check with the teacher. If ability is not the problem, it may be that your child sees the assignment(s) as overwhelming. Break the assignment into more manageable parts. This promotes success. Preview the assignment with your child. Read the directions and check for understanding. Do the first question or problem with your child. This will let him know that it is not so difficult. Provide encouragement at each step. "You do the next three on your own and then I'll come back and check them." Tell your child that you have confidence in his ability to complete the work and do his best. "You did the first one correctly, I bet you can do the next three and get them all right." Be available to answer questions.

Some children resist doing homework because they question the relevance of the assignment. "Why do I have to do that? It's stupid." "I did this last year, I am not doing it again." Unfortunately, not every assignment has equal meaning to every child. Some assignments may be irrelevant and boring. These assignments must be done anyway. You do not have to like it, but you have to do it. This is how the real world operates. We all have aspects of our jobs that are irrelevant and boring. We get use to it.

Teach children to do the worst first. If your child has difficulty with math, do it first. Get it over and feel relieved. The remaining assignments will be less threatening. Doing the worst first makes more sense because your child is more alert mentally.

Students in Fourth Grade and up need a homework buddy. Have your child get the phone number of a friend in each class. If your child has difficulty, forgets an assignment or is sick for a day, he can call the buddy and get information and help. Older students should be taught to use a homework organizer. Many schools have them for sale.

Some children speed through their assignment. This is only a problem if the work is sloppy or inaccurate. If the work is neat and correct, homework is finished for the day. Do not penalize your child for working quickly, as long as he is accurate. If the work is sloppy or inaccurate, have your child redo the assignment. If you anticipate that your child may be a speeder, let him know your rules ahead of time.

Homework Incentives

For most children, the organization and planning strategies discussed above, along with some verbal encouragement are enough to get successful homework habits started. For some children these tactics are not enough. Some children are reluctant. Some children dawdle. These children need stronger incentives.

Use computers and educational software to motivate your children. There are hundreds of software programs that reinforce reading, spelling and math skills. There are interactive encyclopedias, history and science programs on CD ROM. There are on-line research services. These kinds of learning tools are fun and exciting.

Checklists, charts and contracts are good motivators. Have daily, weekly or long term pay-offs. Make a list of the specific activities that your child must follow in order to improve homework habits.

This checklist emphasizes the importance of taking responsibility. Children must realize that school success and doing homework is for them, not you. You already have your education. Do well in school to please yourself. Aim for self reward.

Punishment does not motivate children to do better in school. Punishment does not motivate children to do their best on homework. You can not make your child learn. Motivation to learn and do school work can only be achieved through encouragement and self-discipline. Avoid homework power struggles. Arguments over homework only provide your children with another button to push.

220

	Mon	Tue	Wed	Thur
Write down assignments				
Bring materials home				
Start on time				
Work independently				
Be neat and accurate				
Check your work				
Finish on time				
Turn it in				

Summary

Parents, teachers and children must work cooperatively to develop proper attitudes about learning and homework. Talk with your child's teacher to find out homework policies. Provide your child with enough time and a quiet place to do homework. Be consistent with homework routines. This tells children that school and homework are important. Use a checklist, chart or contract to provide a boost of motivation. Teach children to value their education. It is their future.

Chapter 27

Attention Deficits, Hyperactivity and Behavior

All children can be divided into two groups: hard to raise and harder to raise. Parents often ask why it happens that all of their children are well behaved except one. One child gives them all the grief. I experienced this phenomena with a teenager early in my career. The youngster was fourteen. His father was a very prominent and successful high school principal. His mother was a teacher. There were nine children in this family. Eight were very successful in all aspects of life. He was a delinquent. I am not sure that anyone can fully explain this.

Why is this Child so Difficult?

I have listened to hundreds of parents tell me that their child has been "difficult since birth." Children have different temperaments, skills, interests and abilities. Children also behave differently. Knowing *why* one child is more difficult than the others is not important. Knowing how to handle the situation is important. Difficult children require more from you. They require more of your time and energy. If you want all of your children to be successful and you have one or two children who are particularly hard to raise, it simply means that you will have to be more actively engaged in parenting.

Children with attention deficit disorder (A.D.D.) present a special challenge to parents and teachers. Children with A.D.D. have a poor attention span. They are more impulsive than the average child the same age. Many A.D.D. children are also hyperactive. These children have attention deficit hyperactivity disorder (A.D.H.D.) Treatment for a true A.D.D./A.D.H.D. child typically includes four aspects: medical management, often with medication; educational planning; individual and family counseling; and behavior planning. Here is an example of a behavior plan that can be used with an A.D.D./A.D.H.D. child or any child with special needs.

Planning for Problem Children

Some children have attention deficits and hyperactivity that causes impulsive behavior. Misbehavior may increase due to your child's frustration. Some children have allergies and take medications that affect their moods and may agitate their activity levels. These factors make discipline more difficult. You will need to use careful judgment in deciding what is a misbehavior and what is the effect of the disorder. Be extra positive and consistent during these periods.

Tommy is more active than usual today. He is all over the place. Mom is not sure what to do. She has seen bad days before. She used to make excuses and let Tommy do as he pleased on days like this. She has learned that excuses did not help Tommy learn to control his problem. Now she has a plan. As soon as Mom notices that Tommy is getting too excited or energetic, she takes him aside. "Tommy, you are letting yourself get too active. You need to settle down. You are having a good day so far, I do not want to see you get in trouble. Let me sit with you for a few minutes. I'll read you a story. You take a couple of deep breaths and relax."

Here is Mom's plan. (This plan works well for any child.) She knows that it is important to intervene early. She steps in as soon as she notices Tommy getting active. If she waited until he was out of control, it would be much more difficult to settle him down. Mom has also learned to stay calm. Her calmness influences Tommy to be calm. If she becomes angry or yells, Tommy will get worse. Mom stays with Tommy. She does not just tell him to "settle down" and leave it up to him to settle down by himself. Mom gets Tommy involved with a quiet activity — listening to a story. She asks him to take a few deep breaths to help him relax. This will redirect Tommy. Some children can be redirected by soft music, listening to headphones, listening to a story on cassette tape, or watching television.

After a while, Tommy may only need a cue. A cue is a special signal from a parent that reminds a child to get control. If Mom and Tommy practice this technique consistently each time he gets too excited, they will build a pattern. Tommy will learn to give himself feedback about his activity level. Eventually, he will learn to control himself. I worked with a parent whose cue to her son was, "You need to go to the beach." Her son liked relaxing at the ocean. When he got his signal, he would spread a towel on his bed and lie down and think about being at the ocean.

Remedies at Home

Children like Tommy require consistency. They need structure and routine. Set up schedules for wake up, meal time, job time, homework, TV, playtime, etc. Use a clock or a timer to increase understanding and motivation. Do not change this routine unless you let your child know in advance.

Have specific rules written down. It may be helpful to use a chart or contract. Also have specific consequences written down in advance, punishments as well as incentives.

Use clear language when giving instructions. Demonstrate when you can. Keep it simple. Do not give more than one or two instructions at a time. Ask your child to repeat the instructions to you before he begins to do something.

Provide your child with a quiet place to settle down. You can use this place to read or do homework. Keep this place distraction free.

Stay calm. Children like Tommy can be frustrating. Getting angry usually aggravates the situation.

Many children who are like Tommy need consistent follow through when they do not behave. Time-out has proven to be an excellent way of teaching children with special problems.

Summary

Of course, the ideas in this chapter will work with any child as well as children with special problems. Do not use disabilities as excuses for misbehavior. You will be teaching your child that his weakness is a crutch to use as an excuse the rest of his life. Tommy has an attention deficit disorder. He says, "I can't behave today because I forgot my pill." His parents have taught him that his pill controls his behavior. Children with disabilities need to be taught that the only way to overcome their weakness is by diligence and hard work. Excuses only handicap you more. Children with special problems need special plans, not excuses. Focus your time, energy and consistency on the difficult children and the not-so-difficult children will get through life with your love and discipline.

Chapter 28

Divorce And Behavior

Lisa was the kind of student teachers would call on when they wanted an imaginative answer. She had a reputation for being a child with a cheery and sociable disposition. She was blessed with intelligence, personality and self-confidence. She earned good grades and was a leader among her peers. The world was an exciting place for Lisa. She was optimistic and enthusiastic about her life and her future.

Then her life changed — suddenly and almost completely. She went from honor student to school failure, from cheerful to withdrawn, from leader to loser. She became unsure of herself, inattentive, forgetful and depressed. School was simply not that important to her any more.

What caused this dreadful transformation? Lisa was suffering from an affliction that has no name but strikes as many as eighty percent of the children in some schools. Lisa's parents got a divorce.

How Children Think

When I first met with Lisa, she did everything she could to convince me that she was not having any problems. Lisa's reaction is typical. Like most children who experience the distress of divorce, she could not explain why she was doing poorly in school and she did not want anyone to know she was hurting inside. She did not want to say anything that may intensify the difficulties at home any further. Children see the stress their parents are going through. They fear that exposing their emotions will only add to everyone's misery. This is the reason that most children never talk to their parents about their feelings concerning the divorce. These hidden feelings increase anxiety and weaken a child's ability to perform in school. Additionally, repressed feelings may become the seeds for larger problems later in life.

> "What do you think about your parents getting divorced?"
> "I don't like it."
> "What do you mean?"
> "My mom cries a lot."
> "How does that make you feel?"
> "Sad. I wish she would stop."
> "Do you know why your parents got divorced?"
> "They used to fight a lot."
> "Did they ever fight about you?"
> "Yes."
> "Do you feel it was your fault that your parents got divorced?"
> "Yes. It was all my fault."

With these words, tears filled Lisa's remorseful eyes. I handed her a box of tissues and told her that it was okay to cry. She wept openly for several minutes. She was dumping some of the emotional garbage she had been carrying for months. When she caught her breath, she explained.

> "One time I was standing in front of the TV and my dad yelled at me to move. Then my mom yelled at him to stop yelling at me. Then they got in a big fight and my dad left the house. Two weeks later they told me they were getting a divorce. So I

think they are getting a divorce because of me."

Lisa was overcome by guilt. She was feeling responsible for her parents' divorce. Over half of the children I speak with feel that they were the primary reason for the divorce. They think, "If only I had been better behaved or done a better job on my chores. If only I had kept my room clean or received better grades, my parents would still be together. If I would have been a better child, none of this would have happened." Children blame themselves. This can create overwhelming feelings of poor self-worth, insecurity and depression. When a child feels guilty or depressed, school is simply not that important.

What Happens in School

Twenty-five years ago, the divorce rate was not high enough to merit much attention. It's different today and we have learned a lot along the way. Divorce hurts children and hurt children strike back, sometimes at themselves. Loss, rejection, abandonment, loneliness, fear, guilt, stress, and anger hit hard. Most observers see a connection between the divorce rate and increased rates of gang delinquency, drug use, and dropouts.

Because many of the school children referred to me for learning or behavior problems have experienced a divorce, I have learned a lot about the ways that divorce affects children in school. I have even learned some things about prevention and treatment. Here a some of the things I have found.

Children psychologically bond to both parents. When parents divorce, it is like having half of your personality torn away. Children feel like half of their "self" is missing. These feelings of loss, rejection and abandonment destroy a child's ability to concentrate in school.

These unhealthy feelings increase when parents attack or degrade each other. When one parent says malicious things about the other parent in front of the children, the children worry that these displeasing qualities exist in them. "If dad is a bad person, am I a bad person too? After all, I'm a lot like my dad."

When parents try to get even or outdo each other, the children become confused. I worked with one family where the mother insisted that the children be sheltered from violence. A reasonable request. Dad's favorite weekend activities: Stallone movies on the VCR and afternoon trips to the rifle range. While the parents argued about what was best for the children, the children became divided and emotionally unsteady.

Some children of divorce lose contact with one of their parents. Nathan's parents have been divorced for five years. His father has remarried and has children with his new wife. Over the years, Nathan has gradually lost his relationship with his father.

> "I feel like no one likes me."
> "Do you feel that way because your dad doesn't see you?"
> "Yes."
> "What do you mean?"
> "It must be me. He doesn't like me for some reason."
> "Do you think you have done something wrong?"
> "I must have done something. Maybe I'm a bad kid."
> "Do you think you are a bad kid?"
> "Yes."

"How often do you feel that way?"

"All the time."

"How often do you think about your father?"

"Every day."

Nathan's feelings of rejection and loss cut deep.
He believed that he was a worthless child. He was sure
that his lack of paternal contact meant that he was not
worthy of his father's love and time. He thought about it
every day. His lack of self worth interfered with every aspect of his life. He was afraid to make friends. He was
afraid to do well in school. He was even afraid to get too
close to his mother. If his father did not care, if his father
left him, others would too.

Some children worry about being abandoned by the
caretaking parent. If one parent has left me, how do I know
my other parent won't leave me? Who will take care of me?
This is another reason why children do not talk to their parents about their feelings. A seven-year-old once explained,
"My mom is very angry at my dad. If I tell her how sad I am,
she will get madder. Then she might leave me, too." Children
are afraid to say or do anything that will alienate or provoke
their parents for fear that both may leave.

Anger and aggression are typical reactions to divorce. This is especially true when the parents get angry
at each other. Steven's parents had been divorced for several months. During that time, Steven had been getting
more aggressive at school and at home. What caused the
increased anger and aggression? Steven was angry at his
dad. Angry for leaving. Angry for not spending more time
with him. Angry for having a new girlfriend. Steven did
not direct his anger at dad. That might drive dad away
even more. Steven took it out on peers, because it was

relatively safe to do so. He also took his anger out on his little sister, because she liked dad's new girlfriend.

Steven was also angry at his father because there was not as much money as there once was. "I'm mad because we are poor now. We can't do things like we used to. My dad has all the money." Children soon learn that divorce lowers financial status. Children worry about basic needs and routine. How will we buy food? Will we have to move into a cheaper home? When will I ever get some new clothes? What about the new bike I was supposed to get? Can I still be on the basketball team? Children worry about money and the changes that lower income will bring. It is difficult to think about the French Revolution when you don't know how the bills are going to be paid.

Change frightens children. Often, one parent takes the children and leaves home. They may move in with relatives or into less expensive quarters. For many children, this means a new home, new school, new friends and new stresses. Add this to loss of a parent and radical change in life style and you have the ingredients for an emotional trauma. These changes interfere with success in school.

Some children fear being stolen by an angry or revengeful parent. This fear develops when parents make threats or hostile remarks. "I'll take the kids away from you and you'll never see them again." The thought of never seeing their mother or father again is frightening. This often occurs when one parent is denied access to the children. As a result, children are afraid to walk to school, walk home, or be in a predicament where they might be kidnapped.

Over half of the children I speak with hope their parents will get back together. It is understandable for children to think in this manner. Children want the family to be the way it used to be. This is a fantasy that most children grasp onto regardless of the facts. A college freshman once told me that he frequently thinks about reuniting his parents. They have been divorced since he was six and both parents have been remarried for years. He still hangs on to the possibility.

Delayed Effects

The aftermath of divorce lasts for years. A mother came to speak with me about her seventeen year-old daughter. Melody had always done well in school. She was a well behaved and trustworthy young lady. Within a two month period, it all turned around. Melody quit going to school, became promiscuous, and got involved with drugs. When I spoke with Melody, she knew exactly what was going on inside herself. She was angry at her father. He left her and her mother when Melody was seven. Melody kept hoping he would return. If he did, she wanted to be sure he would be proud of her, so she always did well for him. Then recently, she realized he was never coming back. "So why be good? I decided to stop working so hard and have a good time instead."

It had been ten years since Melody's father left. It took ten years for the hurt and loss to fester to the point where it finally erupted. It took ten years for the effects to become visible. It would be easy to dismiss a ten year-old event as probable cause for a recent change in behavior. I now realize that the impact of divorce may be immediate or may not surface for years. Teachers and other school professionals must be aware of this when working with troubled children. Do not overlook a divorce as influencing a child's behavior or mood just because it happened several years ago. It may still be fresh in the child's mind.

Monday Morning Re-Entry

The most common debilitating effect of divorce is Monday morning re-entry after a weekend with dad (or mom). Many children of divorce see their non-custodial parent only on weekends, usually two weekends a month. Upon returning from the weekend visit, many children go through a period of adjustment that may last for several days. Some children withdraw, daydream and show a lack of motivation. Other children act out, become short tempered, belligerent and oppositional. Some children become vengeful and aggressive.

Several years ago, when divorce was less common, teachers and parents assumed that the Monday-morning re-entry behavior was caused by a weekend of freedom with no limits and no discipline. The popular conclusion was that the children should see less of this parent. It is true that weekend parents have a tendency to indulge their children, however, Monday morning re-entry is the result of something else.

We now realize that Monday morning re-entry is likely caused by seeing too little of the weekend parent. There are at least two reasons for this. First, a weekend is barely enough time to get acquainted with someone on an intimate or affectionate level. Just as the parent and children start warming up to each other, it's over. The children relive the loss of a parent every other Sunday night. Since it takes several days to deal with this loss, the re-entry behaviors result.

Second, many weekend parents feel like outsiders in their children's lives. The parent and children do not see enough of each other to learn each other's likes, dislikes, interests, emotions, or patterns of behavior. Weekend parents do not get to know their children and weekend children do not get to know their parent. The result: the Disneyland syndrome. Weekend parents have a tendency to pack the weekend with expensive, fun filled activities, gifts and junk food. This does two things. It tells the children that this parent is nice. It also eliminates any need for routine discipline. Children do not misbehave when they are being stuffed with goodies and entertainment.

What's the cure? More time with the weekend parent. Increased contact eliminates the feelings of loss and the re-entry behaviors are diminished. More time with the weekend parent also neutralizes the Disneyland effects. As this parent becomes more involved with the children, more routine time will occur. This parent will develop a wider view of the children's lives and will become more committed to all aspects of the children, including discipline. This usually leads to more cooperation and consistency between the parents. The result is a more stable environment for the children. The children end up doing better for both parents and better in school as well.

A Child's Three Wishes

The effects of divorce on children cannot be eliminated, but their impact can be reduced. What follows is a list of optimal circumstances that may not always be easy for parents to accomplish, but are always best for children.

Wish 1. Children should have free access to both parents. They should be able to phone or see either parent without fear of offending the other parent. Children should not have to choose between parents. This creates a lose-

lose situation. Choose one and lose the other. Children need permission to love both parents in front of each parent.

What about the circumstance where one parent is far away? Many absent parents mistakenly believe that the children they left behind are better off without them. Not true. Encourage as much contact as possible. Write letters and make phone calls. Children love E-mail. Mail messages on cassette tape or video tapes. Send pictures. Mail copies of school reports and invitations to events. Visit on holidays and summer vacations. The more contact the better. If a parent refuses contact, explain that it is not the child's fault. Lack of contact does not make the child a worthless person. Provide frequent reassurance by pointing out the lovable qualities in the child.

There are some situations where contact should be restricted. For example, a parent who has abused the children should have supervised visitations. In situations such as this, the children should receive counseling.

Wish 2. Children want consistency in order to feel safe and secure. Parents need to establish similar rules and consequences at both homes. Parents need to periodically discuss and agree on daily routine, such as allowable foods and snacks, movies, bedtime, bathtime, homework, church, etc. A cooperative spirit tells children that both parents are likable people. Children want pleasant parents as much as parents want pleasant children. Consistency gives children balance and helps them adjust to the divorce situation. Better adjustment means better performance in school.

Many single parents feel guilty. Guilty parents have a tendency to give-in to misbehaviors. They make excuses. "It's not his fault. He is confused right now." Giving-in to misbehavior is a mistake. Be consistent. Be understanding and supportive, but do not let children misbehave. Children need limits and consistency.

Wish 3. Children should know that both parents are still involved in their lives. Parents do not divorce their children. Children need dual parenting. This goes beyond joint custody. Children need both parents actively participating in all aspects of their lives, particularly school. Both parents should attend teacher conferences, if not together, then separately. Both parents should attend school functions. They can sit apart or take turns going to events. Dual involvement clearly indicates that both parents believe that school is a priority. This makes doing well in school more important to the child.

What Schools Can Do

Schools have a responsibility to stay in touch with both parents, even if the custodial parent does not like it. Schools should provide a model for best practice. Since children do better when both parents are involved in the education process, schools need to make every effort to include both parents. Send two report cards. Set up two parent conferences. Send two invitations to school events. Call both parents when the child has a good day. This will create a more stable and supportive home-school-home environment.

Teachers should also be aware that children of divorce often exhibit emotional and behavioral problems. Provide support and encouragement during difficult times. Be a good listener. Allow time for the child to talk about feelings. A teacher may be the only adult with whom he is willing to talk.

Blended and Extended Families

Remarriage often creates blended families. A blended family includes children who are his, hers and theirs. There may be several children from different marriages that live together at different times of the week or month or year. It's confusing. That is why it is even more important that parents be consistent in these situations. More consistency means less confusion.

Consistency is important in extended families. I worked with a family where a six-year-old lived with her mother, her uncle, and her two grandparents. She had four parents. Everyone was giving her different messages. Uncle was mister nice-guy. Anything she did was permissible to him. Grandparents were always trying to get her to behave by bribing her with goodies. Mom had to be the heavy. She did all the punishing and yelling and screaming and threatening. When the mother came to me for counseling, I listened during our first session. For our second meeting, we had a group session with mom, uncle, grandma and grandpa. We spent the entire session talking about consistency; rules, bedtime, snacks, etc.

There are many forms of families today. All of them can produce normal, well-behaved and self-disciplined children. Children adjust to most family situations. Their adjustment is faster and healthier when parents are consistent.

Summary

Millions of American children have been hurt by divorce. Until recently, we assumed that the natural flexibility and resiliency built into all children would guarantee their survival. We now know differently. Children must feel good about themselves in order to behave and to perform well in school. Emotional conflict, anxiety, stress and fear interrupt the natural growth process.

Children adjust to divorce better and therefore do better in school when both parents are part of their lives. There is no cure for divorce, but there is treatment. Keep peace between the parents and keep both parents in the children's lives. The greater the harmony between parents, the better the adjustment for the children. It's that simple. I realize that many parents who have been through a hostile divorce are thinking that these suggestions are unrealistic. That may be so. I am writing about what is best for children. What is best for children is consistency between parents.

Chapter 29

Peer Pressure

Billy came home from school with tears in his eyes. He was the only student in his fifth grade class who got 100 on the math test. All his friends teased him. They called him a "school boy." If you want to be popular at school, it's better to be good at football than be good at math.

How Peer Pressure Works

Peer pressure is the influence that children have on each other. Peers can have a positive influence. Sometimes they do. Unfortunately, some peer pressure is negative. There is pressure to join gangs, to drink and do drugs, pressure to have sex, pressure not to do well in school.

Children are susceptible to peer pressure from the time they start school. Peer pressure occurs in the classroom, on the playground, in the cafeteria or anywhere children gather. Being able to withstand negative peer pressure is a problem for children and teenagers.

The message is — be a part of the crowd. Don't stand out. Don't be unique. Be just like everyone else. Don't have the best clothes. Don't have the worst clothes. Don't get the highest grade. Don't get the lowest grade. Be somewhere in the middle.

Most teenagers are their own worst critic. They catastrophize their shortcomings. That's why they spend so much time in front of mirrors. They need to look perfect on the outside because they are confused about the inside. Our society promotes looking perfect. The average American child sees 350,000 commercials by age 16.

"Buy our cereal and be more athletic." "Use our toothpaste and your love will last forever."

From the time they are young, teach your children that happiness comes from the inside, never the outside. Every individual is different. Everyone has strengths and weaknesses, pros and cons, good points and bad points. It's normal to be different. Teach your children to focus on what they do well. Do not dwell on imperfections.

> "Not everyone can be great at soccer. Some people are more athletic than others. You have other strong points. You are very kind. Everyone who knows you likes you. You have a pleasant sense of humor. Your grades are always good. Don't put yourself down about soccer. Do your best and enjoy the game."

Your child's best defense against peer pressure is confidence. Arm your child with self-worth by pointing out strengths and successes. Teach him to have integrity. "You have always been able to stand up for yourself and do what you know is right. You should be proud of yourself for that." This will teach your child to believe in himself and his ability to make choices. Talk to your children about self esteem. Tell them it's all right to feel low about yourself. Teach them to talk to someone when they feel sad or depressed. Let them know they can come to you with any problem.

> "It's okay to be down occasionally. It happens to everyone. When I feel low, talking seems to help. If I talk about what's bothering me, the problem doesn't feel so big. Mom and I talk about problems to each other all the time. It helps us feel better.

You decide what you want to do. No matter what it is, I'll be here if you need me."

Encourage your children to talk to other children about feelings. "I know you have a good friend you can talk to about this. I bet she has the same fears and worries about the dance that you have. Talk with her. You may both feel better."

Remind your children that no one has all the answers. It's normal to feel unsure of yourself at times. When children see that other children feel the way they do, they realize it's common. They don't feel so alone and scared. They don't feel so empty and hopeless.

Let your house be a place for teenagers to hang out. Give them some privacy. Let them listen to music, talk and play games. Whenever you can, compliment the group about their friendship. "I'm glad to see you get along so well. Having good friends makes growing up a little easier." Teach your teenagers to support each other. Be friends with people who like you for what you are. Teach your children to stay away from peers who are critical. "Not everyone has the same sense of right and wrong. Stay away from kids who bring you down and make you feel bad. Let them be the way they are without you. If you can influence them to do better — great — but do not let them influence you to do less."

There may be peer pressures at school that you cannot change. Involve your children with other groups. Get them involved with church groups, scouts, or other groups that are supportive.

Listening Builds Trust

Troubled teenagers say, "I can't talk to my parents. They don't understand me. They don't know anything about me. I don't trust them. They don't trust me."

Successful teenagers say, "I know I can tell my parents anything. They listen to my problems. I'm not afraid to tell them when something has gone wrong. They trust me." Successful children have parents who are good listeners.

When children and teenagers have problems, they need to know they can come to you for help. When they do not feel safe coming to you for help, they often face their problems alone. For some children and teenagers, this is all right. For others, it is not. Many children who cannot face their problems alone try to escape their problems. Common escapes are gangs, drinking, drugs and suicide.

Respect promotes healthy listening. We often show more courtesy to strangers than our children. Are you as polite to your children as you are to your boss or your neighbor? Show respect for your children and they will learn to respect you and themselves. When you speak to your children, show trust, confidence and acceptance. They will do the same.

"I would like to hear what you think."

"I trust your ideas on ...."

"I may not agree with you, but it's good to say what you feel."

"I may not have listened well the last time we talked. I'm sorry. If you will give me another chance, I would like to listen to you now."

Be attentive when your children speak to you. It is easy to be distracted by your surroundings — the television, telephone interruptions, or other children making noise. Anger can be a distraction. It is difficult to pay attention and think clearly when you are upset. It is easy to become preoccupied with your own thoughts — worries about money, mentally reviewing items at work or getting dinner ready.

There were many times when my children wanted to talk to me while I was engrossed in writing this book. It was not always easy to turn away and listen. There were times when I would ask them to wait. "I'm in the middle of an important idea. Can you come back in three minutes?" It is better to be honest than to pretend to listen.

Take care of your distractions and preoccupations and then focus on your child. Look at him. Let him know that you believe talking is important. It may be helpful to find a quiet place where you will be free from interruptions and distractions. Go for a ride or a walk. Go sit in the park. This will emphasize the importance of the communication for both of you. This lets him know that what he says is important. It tells him he can talk to you about anything. This takes practice and commitment. Be open to anything he says. No matter how bizarre or frightening, listen without blame or judgment. If he says something that makes your stomach flip, try clarifying.

How to Clarify and Express Feelings

Clarifying means rephrasing your child's statement. Listen for the hidden feeling or meaning in what your child says. When you think you have it figured out, use clarifying to check your perception. Here is how many parents react.

Lisa: "Trisha is a jerk."
Mom: "Don't talk that way. I have told you
        that before."

The tone of Mom's response is critical. Mom is responding to Lisa's words. Mom's response is closed. It shuts down further communication. Lisa will not say much more about her problem or her feelings.

> Lisa: "Trisha is a jerk."
> Mom: "Are you angry at Trisha?"
> Lisa: "Yes. She told the other girls I like Brian."

In this example, Mom's response is open-ended so Lisa keeps on talking. Mom perceives that Lisa is angry. She checks it out. This lets Lisa know that Mom is listening. Your first perception may not always be correct. Open responses will encourage children to keep talking anyway. Incorrect open responses are better than closed responses.

> Lisa: "Trisha is a jerk."
> Mom: "Are you angry at Trisha?"
> Lisa: "I'm not angry. I'm hurt. She didn't invite me to her party."

Being a good listener means hearing beyond the words. Use clarifying to keep your child talking about his feelings and the problem. Do not respond with criticism, judgment or advice. Keep your opinion to yourself until your child wants to listen. Then use guiding questions to teach your child to think for himself.

Teaching Children to Think for Themselves

Parents enjoy giving their children advice. We like to solve their problems for them. We like to protect them

244

from making a wrong decision. We like to give them the answers. We do not like waiting for them to generate their own alternatives. In most situations, this is harmless. Sometimes it's not. There are times when they need to think for themselves. Your goal is to teach your child to think before acting. "I wish I would have thought about that first." Teenagers need to think for themselves when they face peer pressure, drug and sex decisions, and school problems.

Children need to practice solving their problems when they are young, so they will know how to solve problems when they are teenagers. Rather than provide solutions, teach your children how to generate their own alternatives.

The following questioning technique will allow you to guide your child's thinking while he makes a decision.

What did you do?

What were you supposed to do?
(or What is the rule?)

Did you make the right choice?
(or Was that a good decision?)

What could you have done differently?

What could you do next time?

These questions are suggestions. You may develop your own technique that works as well. Here is a dialogue between Mom and twelve year-old Kayla. This is an example of how to use guiding questions.

Mom:	"What did you do, Kayla?"
Kayla:	"She was teasing me."
Mom:	"Just tell me what you did."
Kayla:	"I hit her."
Mom:	"What's the rule about hitting?"
Kayla:	"But she was calling me names, too."
Mom:	"Did you hit?"
Kayla:	"Yes."
Mom:	"Was that a good decision?"
Kayla:	(Silence.)
Mom:	"What else could you have done besides hitting?"
Kayla:	"I could have walked away"
Mom:	"That's right. That might have been a better choice. Would you be in trouble if you had walked away?"
Kayla:	"No."
Mom:	"Maybe you should try that the next time someone teases you.

Mother would not accept excuses and would not let Kayla distract her. She was teaching Kayla to think about what she did and develop alternatives for the future.

When your child cannot think of alternatives, refrain from giving advice. If you give advice and it does not work, it's your fault. Give suggestions by telling a story. "When I was your age, I had a friend who had a similar situation. She solved her problem by ignoring the kids who were teasing her." This strategy plants the idea. Leave it up to your child to make the choice. (I do not feel this is deceit. I am sure this happened to one of my friends at some point.)

By asking the right questions you can avoid arguments and teach your child how to make better decisions. Here is an example of a case that is more difficult.

Dad: "What happened Kevin?"

Kevin: "Nothing happened."

Dad: "What did you do?"

Kevin: "I said nothing happened."

Dad: "It looks to me like you hit your brother."

Kevin: "Then why did you ask if you already know?"

Dad: "We have spoken about this before. You know that hitting is not permitted in this house. I hope that the next time this occurs, you make a better decision. We can decide what to do about this later."

Dad makes the point about decision making in spite of Kevin's lack of cooperation. Situations like this are common, especially with strong-willed children. Even though Kevin was unwilling to discuss the matter, Dad remained calm. Dad did not start lecturing Kevin about hitting or about being stubborn. Dad recognized that Kevin was not willing to talk. Wisely, Dad did not insist. It is better to wait for Kevin to cool off before talking further. Dad will have more of Kevin's attention.

Summary

Zest for living must exist within yourself. It cannot come from outside sources. Your children learn this from you. Love your children unconditionally and they will learn to do the same. Show each of your children how much you value her or him. "No matter how tough the world out there gets, someone supports me." That's what children need to deal with peer pressure.

Guide children to think for themselves when they are young. Give them choices. Praise them when they make good decisions. Show them where they could improve poor decisions. Help them see alternatives to their decisions and their behavior. Guide your child to think about solutions on his own. Show your child how decisions result in consequences. Teach them the power to choose their future.

Part VI: HOW TO ENJOY BEING A PARENT

Chapter 30

Promise To Appreciate

Anthony doesn't "pee" in the refrigerator anymore. After reading about himself on page one, he said he felt like doing it again just to get even with me for telling the story. Since his bladder capacity is considerably greater than it was ten years ago, I am trying to stay on his good side. We have made it to the fireworks for the past six years. I have learned how to keep dumb threats to myself. Leah eats like a superstar whenever we go out to dinner. She still orders a cheeseburger with fries and a small milk and one straw. I have stopped cursing in parking lots, almost.

Michael no longer has tantrums in the supermarket or anywhere else. He still loves candy. Mrs. Ellis has not taken any more vacations from consistency. Her children are doing quite well in school and at home. Nancie will graduate from high school this year. She has not skipped classes to hide in her closet in four years, as far as we know.

You cannot accuse children of being boring. They will always think of something you are unprepared to handle. Being a parent is demanding. Parenting requires countless sacrifices and continuous hard work. Fortunately, there are many rewards: the pride of achievement, the miracle of growth and development; the warmth and affection. If your children's misbehavior is depriving you of these rewards, you are being cheated. Do not let their misbehavior interfere. You are doing the work without the glory. You are being denied the pleasures of parenting. You deserve to enjoy your children.

Several years ago, I was at a school for profoundly handicapped children. When I got in my car to leave, I decided to write some notes. While I was working, a station wagon drove in and parked in front of me. An elderly gentleman got out. He walked around to the back and opened the hatch. He was struggling with something. Then I realized what it was — a wheelchair. He dragged it to the ground and locked it into position. He rolled the chair to the passenger side, opened the rear door, and reached deep inside. He emerged with his full grown son in his arms. He placed his son's dangling torso in the chair, fastened the strap and wheeled him into school.

My only thought was for my children. How many times had I silently complained about buckling Leah into her car seat? How often was I upset because her arms and legs did not move as quickly as I wanted? It was a painful but revitalizing insight. I made a vow. I promised to appreciate and enjoy my children to the fullest.

All parents want to enjoy their children. Few parents get the enjoyment they deserve. It is easy to appreciate your children when they are cooperative and well behaved. You can spend your time and energy on pleasant endeavors. You do not have to yell and argue. It is difficult to enjoy your children when they misbehave. Misconduct creates tension.

Many parents avoid their children to escape the stress and irritated feelings. They send their children outside to play so they do not have to deal with them. They cannot wait until the children go to bed. They see their children as a burden and resent them. They hope for the day when their children leave home. This is a tragic waste of a precious opportunity. It can be avoided. Take time periodically to review these points.

Ten Principles to Practice

1. Pay off correct behavior, not misbehavior. Reinforce polite requests, not whining, teasing and tantrums. Reinforce calm discussions, not arguments and power struggles.

2. Think before you talk. Say what you mean. Mean what you say. Follow through. Give yourself visual reminders. Reward yourself for being consistent.

3. Expect good behavior from your children. Children must know what you expect from them and what they can expect from you. When children can predict how you behave in given situations, they make better choices.

4. Children believe what you tell them. Coach your children on ways to be successful. Teach your children that effort is essential to success. Use plenty of encouragement. When you encourage your children, they will see that you have faith and confidence in them. Encouragement will help your children face situations with more confidence.

5. Anticipate problems. Tell them the rules in advance. Be specific. Be reasonable. Once you recognize a misbehavior pattern, establish a plan. Spotlight success. Provide support and encouragement. Use charts and contracts to strengthen your plan.

6. Use punishments that teach decision-making and accountability. Children survive reasonable punishments, such as restriction and time-out. Do not punish when you are angry. Do not punish to get even. Relate punishment to your child's decisions. This teaches responsibility.

7. Begin teaching responsibility and decision-making when your children are young. Prepare your children to live in the real world. Be strict but positive. Children need limits and structure. Children need ground rules. They need consistency. Children see these qualities as an expression of your love and concern.

8. Love your children regardless of their behavior. Focus on your children's positive qualities. Teach your children to seek self reward — to feel good about doing the right thing. Look for praiseworthy decisions. Teach your children to like themselves. Teach them to understand their weaknesses and accept their faults. Use yourself as an example. They will learn to admit their shortcomings to others. As a result, their weaknesses will have less power in their lives.

9. Support yourself, even when others sit in judgment. Do not let your children push your button. Be strong. Control your own behavior to be a good model. Your children learn from you.

10. Provide a healthy and pleasant family climate. Emphasize each other's strengths. Accept each other's weaknesses. Talk about values and goals. Your children will learn to come to you with their problems. This will come in handy when they are teenagers.

Final Thoughts

Being a successful parent is hard work. Developing well-behaved children requires courage and patience. Trust yourself. You know what is best for your children. Concentrate on the real issues: mental health, happiness, self-respect and love of others.

Some parents believe that love alone will create delightful children. Love is essential, but it does not guarantee good behavior. Misbehavior is not pleasant. There is a better way. Practice the ideas presented in this book.

You have a right to enjoy being a parent. Do not let your children's misbehavior keep you from enjoying them. Take action. Plan to change the misbehavior and then have fun. Laugh and play and get involved with your children. It will keep you feeling young. These are the most valuable years of your life.

Free Newsletter Offer

Thank you for purchasing this book. You are entitled to receive our upcoming newsletter free of charge for one year. The newsletter will be used to inform you of new child rearing strategies as well as answer your questions.

If you have a specific question about your child's behavior that was not answered in this book, please feel free to mail your question to me at the address below. I will try to answer your question in our newsletter.

Please send your name and address or e-mail address to:

Newsletter Offer
Greentree Publishing
P.O. Box 27672
Tempe, Az   85285-7672

Index

P

R

S

T

W

Y

<u>Order Information</u>

How To Behave
So Your Children Will, Too!
New Products:

How To Behave So Your Children Will, Too!
Workbook   *   Video   *   Audio

Other New Audio Programs:
How Successful Parents Behave
The Ten Most Common Parenting Mistakes

Sal Severe, Ph.D.
Greentree Publishing
P.O. Box 27672
Tempe, Arizona 85285-7672
Include your name and return address
Or
Use the *Order Form* or *Gift Order Form*
on the next two pages.
Or
Call 1-800-866-5208
Or
E-mail: greentreepub@earthlink.net
and request an order form

262

Order Form

How To Behave So Your Children Will, Too!

Name: _____

Address: _____

City: _____ State: _____ Zip: _____

Mail your check for $24.45 ($21.95 plus $2.50 shipping) to:

Greentree Publishing
P.O. Box 27672
Tempe, Az. 85285-7672

Or fax your order to: 602-820-1011

Customer Signature: _____

Print Name: _____

Phone Number (___) _____

Card number: ☐☐☐☐ ☐☐☐☐ ☐☐☐☐ ☐☐☐☐

Master Card ☐ Visa ☐

Exp. Date: ☐☐ ☐☐

(cut here or photocopy)

Gift Order Form

We will gift wrap *How To Behave So Your Children Will, Too!*
and include a card from you at no extra cost.

Send to:

Name: _____

Address: _____

City: _____

State: _____ Zip: _____

From:

Name: _____

Address: _____

City: _____

State: _____ Zip: _____

Mail your check for $24.45 ($21.95 plus $2.50 shipping) to:

Greentree Publishing

P.O. Box 27672

Tempe, Az. 85285-7672

Or fax your order to: 602-820-1011

Master Card ☐ Visa ☐

Customer Signature: _____

Print Name: _____

Phone Number: ( ) _____

Card number: ☐☐☐☐ ☐☐☐☐ ☐☐☐☐ ☐☐☐☐

Exp. Date: ☐☐ ☐☐

Do you have an entertaining story about your children?

All of the stories in this book were given to me by parents who have attended my seminars. If you have a story that illustrates a lesson for parents, I would like to hear from you. I may use your example in my next book or in future workshops. Please send your story to the address below.

Please contact me if you are interested in scheduling a speaking engagement such as a lecture, seminar or extended workshop. I have provided training for schools, church groups, preschools and day care centers, special parent interest groups, PTA's, and numerous human resource departments.

You can also contact me if you are interested in attending a seminar or workshop in your area or if you are interested in being on our mailing list. We will soon be producing audio and video tape training programs.

For information on parenting workshops
or book sales call 1-800-866-5208,
or write to:

Sal Severe, Ph.D.
Greentree Publishing
P.O. Box 27672
Tempe, Arizona 85285-7672

Are you an educator?

I am currently working on **How To Behave So Your Students Will, Too!** This book is written for teachers or anyone who manages groups of children. This book is designed to show you how to get the best behavior from your class without feeling exhausted at the end of every day. If you are a teacher, child care provider, counselor, psychologist or principal, this book will be a valuable resource.

I am always looking for good stories that illustrate solutions for children's problems. If you have a story or example about child behavior, classroom management or academic interventions, please send it to me. If I use your example, you will be credited for your submission.